"With the mind of a professor and the heart of a pastor, Terry Wardle takes the reader deeper into the issues of the heart and the soul. The useful integrative and reflective exercises at the end of each chapter are particularly valuable and the readable style will be appreciated. I highly recommend *From Broken to Beloved* for those who want to get in touch with the most personal side of their life, as well as for professionals and practitioners who desire to assist others along this pilgrim journey."

—**Dr. Martin Sanders,** Director of Doctor of Ministry, Alliance Theological Seminary; Founder and President, Global Leadership, Inc.

"What a stunning book! Writing with grace and wit, Wardle makes following Jesus eminently evocative, clear, and practical. Centuries ago Gregory of Nyssa insisted that 'concepts create idols; only wonder understands.' For those who have been exhausted by concept-driven discipleship, this book is a timely invitation to stand in awe and wonder of God."

—**Karlo V. Bordjadze,** Team Leader of CRU, Ohio State University; Adjunct Professor, Ashland Seminary; author of *Darkness Visible*

"*From Broken to Beloved* is a powerfully profound book that truly has the anointed handprint of God. The redemptive words within these pages along with Terry's transparency as he vulnerably shares stories of his own brokenness, captivates the reader, bringing them into the healing presence of God. This book could not have come at a better time in my healing journey. God used Terry's words to bring me into a deeper place of reflecting on my own trauma, brokenness, and redemption. I was elevated into a new level of freedom as I was reminded that I am not alone in this journey. That I no longer need to wear the grave clothes of shame as my past does not define me because I am a new creation in and through Christ. I was able to fully embrace that I am a daughter of the Most High and I am a beloved child of God. *From Broken to Beloved* is healing to the shattered soul and has true resurrection power."

—**Alison Vorlicky,** CEO, Wrecked to Redeemed Ministries

"Terry Wardle paves the way for the reader to know and experience spiritual awakening as repeatable and ongoing. With his honest approach and vulnerable life stories, Terry freely shares his own journey of brokenness and struggle, which leads to being known as the Beloved. *From Broken to Beloved* offers practical awareness exercises after each chapter to gently lead the reader to experience God's presence as the place of transformation. I have known Terry for many years as a man who lets his life speak, and his passionate desire for more of God has awakened my heart and countless other people's hearts to want to know God as he does. I highly recommend this book to awaken your longing to experience life as the Beloved. You won't be disappointed."

—**Dr. Wanda Walborn,** Associate Professor of Spiritual Formation, Alliance Theological Seminary; author of *Spiritual Journey: Can I Really Get Close to God?*

"Terry's humble and confessional writing opens our heart to God and others as we read. God is irresistibly attracted to the contrite of heart; authentic humility begins with honesty. Terry's honesty is refreshing. He doesn't just leave us open and vulnerable though, he leads us to experience and encounter the tenderness of God where our hearts can find a remedy. There are some broken places in our souls that God cannot heal with his power in a moment, but only with his tenderness over time. Linger with the experiences that are in the book. Terry is a trustworthy pastoral guide who can help you make the journey *From Broken to Beloved*."

—**Dr. Rob Reimer,** author of *Soul Care*

"How does a person change from someone who is convinced that they are inadequate and broken to an individual who knows they are valued and loved? Terry Wardle is clear that hard work and achievements will never bring about such a change, but an encounter with God certainly will! In *From Broken to Beloved*, Dr. Wardle offers a simple and doable spiritual exercise using the acronym RING (Remain in the light, Imagine prophetically, Notice, and Give thanks). I recently completed an 8-week spiritual direction group with four ladies using another of Dr. Wardle's spiritual exercises—the 3 Rs (Rest, Receive, and Respond) described in *Every Breath We Take*—and I became an eye witness to four journeys of transformation. I am completely confident that this new book with all it has to offer and unpack will be equally amazing and another bright torch lighting the way on the journey to wholeness."

—**Sharon E. Siler,** EdD, Executive Director, The Healing Place Center for Counseling and Spiritual Formation, Mechanicsville, Virginia

From
BROKEN
to
BELOVED

In memory of Della Saunders—
an African American saint who
lived on the battlefield for her Lord

From
BROKEN
to
BELOVED

A Journey of Awakening

TERRY WARDLE

LEAFWOOD
P U B L I S H E R S
an imprint of Abilene Christian University Press

FROM BROKEN TO BELOVED

A Journey of Awakening

LEAFWOOD
P U B L I S H E R S

an imprint of Abilene Christian University Press

Copyright © 2021 by Terry Wardle

ISBN 978-1-68426-471-1 | LCCN 2021013727

Printed in the United States of America

Scripture quotations, unless otherwise noted, are from The Holy Bible, New International Version®, NIV®. Copyright © 1973, 1978, 1984, 2011 by Biblica, Inc.® Used by permission. All rights reserved worldwide.

Scripture quotations marked NKJV are taken from the New King James Version®. Copyright © 1982 by Thomas Nelson. Used by permission. All rights reserved.

Scripture quotations noted NLT are taken from the Holy Bible, New Living Translation, copyright ©1996, 2004, 2007, 2015 by Tyndale House Foundation. Used by permission of Tyndale House Publishers, Inc., Carol Stream, IL 60188. All rights reserved.

Scripture quotations noted The Message taken from The Message. Copyright © 1993, 1994, 1995, 1996, 2000, 2001, 2002. Used by permission of NavPress Publishing Group.

Scripture quotations marked TLB are taken from The Living Bible copyright © 1971 by Tyndale House Foundation. Used by permission of Tyndale House Publishers Inc., Carol Stream, Illinois 60188. All rights reserved. The Living Bible, TLB, and the Living Bible logo are registered trademarks of Tyndale House Publishers.

Scripture quotations noted ESV are from The ESV® Bible (The Holy Bible, English Standard Version®) copyright © 2001 by Crossway, a publishing ministry of Good News Publishers. ESV® Text Edition: 2016. All rights reserved.

Published in association with the literary agency of Ann Spangler and Company, 1415 Laurel Ave. SE, Grand Rapids, MI 49506.

LIBRARY OF CONGRESS CATALOGING-IN-PUBLICATION DATA
Names: Wardle, Terry, author.
Title: From broken to beloved : a journey of awakening / Terry Wardle.
Description: Abilene, Texas : Leafwood Publishers, 2021. | Includes bibliographical references.
Identifiers: LCCN 2021013726 (print) | LCCN 2021013727 (ebook) | ISBN 9781684264711 (trade paperback) | ISBN 9781684269280 (ebook)
Subjects: LCSH: Christian life. | Spiritual formation.
Classification: LCC BV4501.3 .W3618535 2021 (print) | LCC BV4501.3 (ebook) | DDC 248.4—dc23
LC record available at https://lccn.loc.gov/2021013726
LC ebook record available at https://lccn.loc.gov/2021013727

Cover design by ThinkPen Design, LLC | Interior text design by Strong Design, Sandy Armstrong

Leafwood Publishers is an imprint of Abilene Christian University Press
ACU Box 29138 | Abilene, Texas 79699 | 1-877-816-4455 | www.leafwoodpublishers.com

22 23 24 25 26 27 / 7 6 5 4 3 2

CONTENTS

AWAKENING
TO THE WONDER
INSIDE YOU

AWAKENING

1

The moments that transform a life come from spiritual awakening, not personal achievement. It took me a long time to learn that. I spent years exhausting myself trying to achieve. Early in life, the world convinced me that performing would bring life's greatest gifts—security, significance, love, belonging, and purpose. But that promise was never kept. On a path to meaning, I have come to realize that achievement is the gift that keeps on taking, robbing anyone who embraces it of a clear vision of the wonder placed in our hearts by God before time began. I wish I had known that years earlier.

My experiences of spiritual awakening have reached back across the years and redeemed parts of my journey that didn't go well. Because of that, I now see that the narrative arc of my life has always been bending toward wholeness because Jesus has been leaning on me all the time, whether I knew it or not, whether I liked it or not!

Awakening has opened my eyes to see that God's grace is far more lavish than I dared imagine. His love, poured out upon the battered and bruised (and who among us is not battered and bruised?), accomplishes a redemptive miracle that goes beyond anything I could earn or accomplish.

Too often, models of Christian discipleship have prioritized what we need to *do* rather than who we already *are*. Pastors can fall into the trap of focusing on rules, rituals, and religious obligations, uttering warnings that often feel like threats. No wonder we think we have to check off an endless list of spiritual achievements so we can be secure with God! This performance-based "Good News," which is not good news at all, is exhausting, harsh, and harmful.

Fortunately, there is such a thing as "Good News," and it is rooted in a breathtaking gospel, scandalous because of the grace God offers to his wandering children.

If you haven't yet experienced the truth that God loves you lavishly, unconditionally, and eternally, let me assure you that it is possible to awaken to it. There are steps you can take to position yourself for an experience of God that will transform your sense of both who he is and who you are because of your relationship to Christ. The first step involves saying yes to the transforming grace God is extending to you daily, whether you recognize his presence in your life or not.

God's love is not simply a theological concept you need to understand. His love can be experienced. There can be moments in time when you actually awaken to its presence due to the work of his good Spirit, who was sent by Jesus to help you sense and surrender to Love's embrace.

God has endowed you with gifts of grace, given before you drew your first breath. In an age of put-down, rejection, exclusion, and prejudice, he invites you to come alive to the wonder his love has already placed inside of you. God invites you to join him on a journey of awakening that moves you from broken to beloved.

Are you aware that you are evidence of God's creative genius? You are a reflection of your Father in heaven—his living and breathing masterpiece, his work of art. You are a person who has been created in his image.

It may seem hard to believe, considering how much we've been pounded on for not measuring up, but it is true. Deep within, smothered beneath all the wounds, lies, and losses you've experienced and far below the ugliness of bad behavior, abides the wonder of your true self. Your Father's great desire is to awaken you to that wonder.

This is why Christ crossed the universe, became one of us, and took on evil at Calvary. Jesus entered our world to wash away everything that is not part of God's original design in order to release the beauty he put in place before time began.

It's taken me a long time to realize that wonder is never discovered through achievement. It happens when you experience spiritual awakening, initiated by the Father, made possible through Christ, and empowered by the Holy Spirit working in your life. Spiritual awakening is not a one-time event but something repeatable and ongoing. It demands nothing more than that you position yourself for life-altering encounters with God's lavish love.

Concepts Will Never Be Enough

Though I hope to increase your understanding of God's design for you, I realize that reading alone will never lead to your transformation. Awakening begins when you learn how to position yourself to encounter the presence of God.

Be patient with what I am about to write. You may be tempted to throw the book through a window. But give me a chance. Here goes. I don't believe reading the Bible changes anyone. Neither do I think that going to church, praying, singing hymns, or performing a host of other religious activities changes anyone. There—I said it!

What I do believe, and why I regularly read my Bible, go to church, pray, worship, and embrace many other spiritual exercises and activities is that doing so *positions* me to be changed. God is present, often in small ways, sometimes in big ways, when I do these things. When he awakens me to his presence, his presence is what changes me. I'm not changed because I read my Bible. Rather, I'm changed because God shows up while I'm reading my Bible and he touches me.

I play a part of course. I need to position myself where God has been known to show up. God chooses the when, the where, and the degree to which he touches my life as I wait for him there. My part is to stay open to whatever the Spirit is doing. God is the One who does the transforming. It is not my performance that matters but rather my positioning.

Encounters with God, whether small or great, open you more and more to the transforming power of his amazing love, to his lavish grace, and to the hidden wonder that he has placed inside of you. Whether you accept it or not, you would do well to allow God to unleash the treasures of his creative workmanship within you.

The chapters that follow will each end with a spiritual exercise that will help to position you for an experience of presence and grace. If you embrace each exercise, you will make room for God to act upon your life. Whether whisper or wind, I believe he will make you aware of his presence. Awakening will begin to happen, and as it does, the wonder will emerge.

How to Best Position Yourself

Spiritual exercises essentially have one main purpose. They position you to experience the presence of God. You don't practice spiritual activities to prove your devotion or to check off a list of spiritual achievements you think will please God.

When embraced properly, spiritual exercises can open up a space and time for God to work. When he does, awakening increases, and the wonder of your true self begins to emerge. For spiritual exercises to work well, here are some things to keep in mind.

Find a Quiet Place

Spiritual exercises work best in a space that's free from noise and distraction. Choose a comfortable place of solitude, free from interruptions.

Consider how this worked in Jesus's own life. He made a habit of slipping away to meet with the Father, as he did at the Garden of Gethsemane on the Mount of Olives. In Mark 6:31 he even invited his disciples to come away with him to a quiet place in order to experience much-needed rest. Similarly, when you slip away to be with God, your special place can become a sacred space, a sanctuary where awakening can happen more readily.

Pay Attention to Posture

In C. S. Lewis's *The Screwtape Letters*, a fictitious conversation takes place between the young demon Wormwood and his uncle, Screwtape: "My dear Wormwood . . . At the very least, they [humans] can be persuaded that the bodily position makes no difference to their prayers; for they constantly forget, what you must always remember, that they are animals and whatever their bodies do affects their prayers."

This is a sound principle. Find a posture that brings your whole self to attention. Sitting upright, feet on the floor, hands open toward heaven are signals to my soul that I am positioning myself to meet the Lord. Kneeling, lying prostrate on the floor, extending arms in cruciform, or standing with arms raised—each posture communicates that I am anticipating the presence of Love and am ready for awakening.

Practice Deep Breathing

There is a passage in Job that connects the spirit within a person with the very breath of God (Job 32:8). This relationship between breath and the presence of God is nuanced throughout Scripture. It has been suggested by scholars that the name "Yahweh" is actually the sound we make when breathing in and out.

The simple act of breathing can become a constant reminder that your life is hidden in God. So it's important to pay attention to breath whenever you are doing a spiritual exercise. Start by breathing in deeply through your nostrils, hold it, then exhale slowly through your mouth. Do this several times as you begin the exercise. Slow, deep breathing can lower tension in your body as well as raise your awareness—two great benefits when seeking to experience the presence of the Lord.

Embrace Stillness

"Be still, and know that I am God" (Ps. 46:10). Experiencing God and the spiritual discipline of stillness go hand in hand. Since the Father often connects with us through whispers, impressions, gentle nudges, and that still, small voice, you must grow in your ability to step away from noise in order to experience God's promised awakenings. This does not come easily, given the many distractions we battle. The world comes at us loud and fast. But in time, as you move into your sacred space in a posture of expectation, stillness will settle in upon you.

Invite the Holy Spirit to Help You

Your heavenly Father never intended for you to walk this life in your own strength. It is simply too difficult. The presence of evil and the trials that daily come your way make life too challenging to be without a divine ally. Jesus gave you the Holy Spirit, the Helper, to stand with you as counselor, comforter, advocate, and friend. Fortunately, the Holy Spirit does his best work whenever you feel weak. Just cry out to him. In fact, one of the prayers he loves to answer is only one word long: "Help!"

Find your quiet place, assume a posture of receptivity, take a few deep breaths, and simply pray, "Come, Holy Spirit. Make me aware of your presence." Keep inviting his presence as you inhale and exhale. Very soon you will discover that the Helper is already there, ready and willing to lead you into the awakenings you desire.

Stay in the Present Moment

If you are like I am, your thoughts will tend to focus on what has happened in the past that disturbed you or what might happen in the future that could derail you. That past/future focus leaves us perpetually anxious. I know. In fact, I often tell people I have a PhD in anxiety. Jesus warned about this in the Sermon on the Mount, admonishing his followers not to worry about tomorrow but to seek the kingdom of God present in the now (Matt. 6:25–34).

God abides in the present moment and wants to meet you there. As a wise cartoon character once quipped, "The past is history, and the future is a mystery. All we have is the gift of right now. That is why it's called *the present*." Wow! Great stuff.

When you sense your focus shifting to what *has* happened or what *might* happen, don't be hard on yourself but gently ask the Holy Spirit to bring your attention back to right here, right now.

The present moment is where you can experience the Father's love. As you engage in the exercises, try to focus on the fact that the Lord is already present with you.

The spiritual awakening I am talking about will change the way you view yourself and will impact the way you see others, regardless of gender, race, class, age, or creed. Awakening to the wonder God has placed within you will help you see the wonder in every person who crosses your path.

DECIDING TO RING

At the end of each chapter, you will have the opportunity to spend time engaging in a spiritual exercise that I call RING. This is an awareness exercise that will position you to experience God's presence. It has the potential to birth a spiritual encounter with God that leads to deeper transformation. Remember: your job is simply to position yourself before the Lord by engaging in the exercise. It is up to the Father to meet you there. If you are patient and open to his presence, awakenings will begin to occur. The acronym RING involves a four-step process described as follows:

Remain in the Light
Imagine Prophetically
Notice
Give Thanks

Remain in the Light

When life's difficulties weigh you down, when you feel surrounded by voices that shout "You are not enough," and when the accuser taunts you about your inadequacies, it is easy to auger into a dark hole of self-contempt and self-judgment. At such times you must resist the temptation to isolate yourself from God. Instead, you must remain in the light of his presence as Jesus taught in John 15. Remember that Paul encouraged you to set your mind on things that are above—whatever is true, noble, right, pure, lovely, admirable, excellent, and praiseworthy (Phil. 4:8).

At the end of each chapter, you will be given a Scripture passage that is to act as your focal point. After properly positioning yourself, you will read a specific truth from the Bible that focuses on a truth about God's love for you, or an important fact about the wonder he has placed inside you. The truths listed will not be about something that may *someday* be true of you, but blessings that are *already* present within your life because of the Father's generous and lavish love.

These endowments of grace are yours now and forever. They are rock-solid truths about the wonder that abides in your heart right now. You will be encouraged to read and meditate on these truths with the help of the Holy Spirit. Once you have spent some time *remaining in the Light*, you will move prayerfully to the next step in the spiritual exercise.

Imagine Prophetically

It's not enough to simply hear or memorize a truth of scripture. You must *experience* it. Experiencing is what actually hardwires a truth into our brain. One powerful way to do that is by engaging your imagination. Einstein said that "Logic can get us from A to B, but imagination can take us around the world." He also pointed out that we are not experiencing a failure of knowledge in the world, but a failure of imagination.

Though imagination is a gift from God, most of us misuse it by spending countless hours imagining either what has gone wrong or could go wrong. This negative use of the imagination adds tension and sometimes illness to our lives. Learning to engage imagination around spiritual truth, on the other hand, can bring new levels of joy and peace to our lives.

This is where you need to invite the Holy Spirit to take over your imagination, using it to help you "see" the specific truth listed at the end of each chapter. Allow the Spirit to show you, like a moving picture in your mind, the specific scripture upon which you are focusing.

Let me give you an example of how this can work. Kelley was a young woman who carried a deep wound because her father abandoned her as a child. She wrestled daily with feelings of insecurity and rejection. Those feelings in turn damaged her relationship with her husband and children. During one of our meetings, I turned to Ephesians to show her that she was actually a chosen child of God. Simply reading that text had little effect on her. But I didn't stop with reading the passage. Instead, I went on to invite her to allow the Holy Spirit to "show" her that she was chosen.

It took Kelley a while to surrender to the process, but once she did, it was transformational. Asking God to sanctify her imagination, she began to "see" herself in a great ballroom filled with people dancing and having a wonderful time. As she sat alone in the corner watching everyone else, she felt abandoned and unwanted. Suddenly, she saw the crowd divide as Jesus walked up to her, extended his hand, and began to dance with her. Tears streamed down her face as she cried, "Jesus chose me!" This single

Holy Spirit-directed moment awakened her not only to the reality of Christ's love but also to her value in his eyes.

Imagination can become the birthplace of deep experiences of the presence of Love.

Notice

Paraphrasing the Scottish psychiatrist R. D. Laing, I want to emphasize that our lives are limited not simply because we fail to take notice, but even more because *we fail to notice that there is anything to notice in the first place.* In fact, noticing can be one of the most important spiritual disciplines we can practice. Unfortunately, our preoccupation with what has happened in the past and with what might happen in the future keeps us blinded to the wonder embedded in every present moment.

Have you ever driven a short distance only to realize you couldn't recall the journey? I've done that on the way to work, so preoccupied that I cannot remember if I stopped at a light, kept the speed limit, or even passed a friend stranded along the side of the road. Instead, I've been lost in my own thoughts, simply driving on autopilot.

God has given each of us amazing abilities to notice through seeing and hearing, taste and touch, smell and body response, spirit and intuition. Each of these gifts can help you become more aware in the present moment. Here are several suggestions for noticing that go along with the RING spiritual exercise.

After "Remaining in the Light" and taking time to "Imagine Prophetically," spend time focusing upon five specific focal points of awareness. Ask the Holy Spirit to quicken your attentiveness as you:

- Notice the presence of the Holy Spirit with you as you do this exercise.
- Notice the feelings that arise as you imagine the specific truth being highlighted.
- Notice your body response, becoming aware of any tension that leaves your body as you focus on the light.
- Notice what you sense the Lord saying to you in the exercise, writing down what you are experiencing in a journal.
- Notice throughout the day the ways in which God reinforces what he has said in the exercise. Pay attention to what you see, hear, taste, touch, smell, read, or experience. You will find that the Lord is always speaking, wanting you to notice how he feels about you, reinforcing the central truth that he loves you and that you are a wonder.

Give Thanks

Did you know that gratitude is a natural antidepressant? Scientists have discovered that giving thanks releases chemicals in the brain that can lift our spirits. It can also give birth to generosity in a person who is otherwise self-absorbed.

The writers of Scripture were thousands of years ahead of today's researchers. The Bible, especially the Psalms, emphasizes the importance of gratitude and giving thanks. Even a casual reading of God's Word reveals that gratitude is a cherished virtue of the kingdom of God.

Close out your RING experience by giving thanks to the Lord for blessings great and small. It will not be difficult to lift up five or six blessings that have been especially important to you.

Do you remember the story of the ten lepers (Luke 17:11–19)? Ten men were healed, but only one came back to thank Jesus. The Lord connected his act of gratitude to faith itself. I would suggest that gratitude for what the Lord is showing you about his love, and the wonder inside of you, will strengthen and increase what you believe about God and discover about yourself. In some miraculous way, gratitude is able to seal the truth more deeply within your life.

I hope these guidelines will enrich your experience. As you read the pages that follow, you may be tempted to finish a chapter and then jump past the spiritual exercise in order to start the next chapter without engaging RING. I urge you to resist that impulse and to remember that simply understanding the concepts in this book will not be enough to bring transformation. When you marry understanding with experience—that's when transformation occurs.

Don't miss this journey of awakening! It will forever transform the way you view God and the wonder that he has planted right inside of you as his beloved.

2

THE WONDER
INSIDE YOU

I was sitting in my office midmorning, handling routine paper-
work when I heard Mike asking my assistant if I was in. I felt
upbeat about his unexpected arrival, anticipating lively conversation and maybe even a few laughs.

The senior pastor at First Presbyterian Church in Ashland,
Ohio, Mike is young, bright, and dedicated, with a great sense of
humor. But as he rounded the corner, I realized this wasn't going
to be a social call. His face was dark and drawn, his eyes a pool of
sadness and grief. He struggled with words he didn't want to say,
with a message he never imagined he would deliver.

What Mike told me that morning seemed straight out of the
theater of the absurd. Incomprehensible. Shock, sadness, and
anger collided in a sudden explosion of disbelief in my heart.

We stared at each other in stunned silence. A strikingly lovely
member of our community had died that morning—at her own hand.

This beautiful, bright young woman was only twenty-seven
years old. A star athlete while in college, she had worked in campus

ministry at our local university, loving students and pointing them toward the beauty of Christ. They adored her. Students invariably described her with words like *safe, encouraging, accepting, compassionate,* and *attentive.* My encounters with her had always left me concluding, "What a gift!"

But there was another truth about her. She could never see the wonder inside herself that was obvious to everyone else. She obsessed on what was broken, unable to grasp just how beloved she was by God and countless others. The weight of emotional wounds, voices from the past screaming that she had to measure up, the deeply held belief that there was something fundamentally wrong with her, as well as diagnosable mental struggles, shouted too loudly in her soul, and in the end she killed the pain in apparently the only way she knew how, choosing to step out of this life once and for all.

Why would she do this? Why was it so difficult for her to see what took most people's breath away whenever they spent time with her? Why have other members of God's family chosen this same path?

How can it be that God's children, who daily host the presence of God's Spirit in their lives, struggle with issues of self-worth and self-image? For some of us, the battle is a low-level, nagging problem we have learned to live with and hide. Though it can be exhausting and frustrating, we fail to realize how much it robs us of present-moment possibilities.

For others, the struggle rages far more openly, pushing them to silence the voices of contempt and hopelessness by whatever pain-killing strategy they find effective—addiction, dependency, disorder, dysfunction, and sadly, even death.

At the news of this young woman's death, my sadness and sorrow went deep quickly, understandably. What frightened me was the anger that began rising up in my soul like a dormant volcano suddenly awakening with destructive force. I was furious, and the rage boiling up from within frightened me. What was happening? I wasn't immediately sure.

Toxic Anger

There was a time when anger was a serious problem for me.

Do you remember the flimsy balsa wood airplanes with a large rubber band running the length of the fuselage, connected to a red plastic propeller? Yes? Then you will also recall that you had to twist the propeller until the rubber band was in knots, sometimes double and triple knots, then raise it toward the sky and let it fly. The more twists, the longer the flight; the more knots, the farther the airplane would soar.

That rubber band, with double and triple knots, is a perfect metaphor for the anger that had been twisted up inside me for years. Despite appearing calm and even-tempered, I could react to the slightest provocation with the kind of anger that would put even the bold back on their heels. Sadly, in defending myself with such intensity, I hurt the people I loved most.

Early in my life, anger became the bodyguard hiding hurt and pain from my childhood. It was the toxic fruit of unprocessed emotional ruptures that desperately needed healing. In a story told elsewhere in my memoir *Some Kind of Crazy*, I share how vulnerability and grace positioned me for transformation. One result of encountering Jesus in the past was the gradual neutralizing of not only the chronic pain of unhealed wounds but also the anger that had built up inside. That anger would sometimes release unpredictably, like the explosion of a steam engine without a pressure valve. It was not a short journey to peace. In fact, I'm still on that path. But meeting Christ in the pain of the past has permitted the bodyguard of anger to stand down.

Over the last several years, my son has commented that he has watched God do a work in my life, moving me from a "son of thunder" to an "apostle of love." That may be overstated, but I like hearing him say it. It has become my prayer as I've been amazed that the journey with Jesus has brought good changes and sweet truth that everyone around me seems happy to enjoy. Peace in the present moment came only because God helped me deal with unhealed wounds of the past.

Hearing about this young woman's death, however, was shattering, and I felt enraged. This was robbery of the highest degree, and somehow, in some small way, I felt compelled to push back, to try saying something, doing something that might not only awaken people to the web of lies that drives all self-contempt and judgment but also awaken God's people to the wonder inside us all. There was anger, but somehow it was different this time—possibly even righteous.

A Dark Harmony of Voices

I have come to realize that there is an all-out assault aimed with laser-precision at God's beautiful children. This assault is often accompanied by undetected background music, subliminal for sure, but yet a screeching harmony comprised of four ugly voices constantly screaming, "You don't measure up!" "There's something wrong with you!" "If people really knew you, they would reject you!" "You're not enough!" "You're fundamentally unlovable!"

This off-key composition of darkness is louder some days than others but serves as the score that daily sets a destructive emotional landscape to many people's lives—Christians most of all.

I have struggled with these destructive tones myself and have sat with countless brothers and sisters in the faith who, in the secrecy of private moments, have confessed the same. It can be exhausting. They dare not say much about the struggle in church gatherings for fear of being faith-shamed. But the battle is real and the toll more than some can bear.

The first voice in this four-part harmony of disrespect belongs to the evil one. He sings lead. Every day, in countless ways, Satan and his minions work to steal, destroy, and in some cases kill God's beloved children. His tools are deception, and his target is individual self-worth. He fights ruthlessly to keep God's children from seeing the masterpiece that is placed inside. The Prince of Darkness hates God's light and is hell-bent on stomping it out, especially when he sees it in the hearts of those who belong to God. He has declared war, and people made in God's image are ground zero. Too many of God's own do not recognize the fight or know how to combat the assault. They simply limp ahead in step with the music of the night.

Second, and most sadly, many of us sing right along, adding our own voices to the refrain. Self-judgment and self-contempt are rampant in the community of Christ. When the night is dark and the wind is howling, we tend to define ourselves by frailties and struggles, by mistakes and wanderings, sure that something is fundamentally wrong at the core of our being. We seem incapable of grasping the fact that we are new creations in Christ. We hear the words but have our doubts. Over time, we wish we were something other than who we believe we are; and by echoing self-contempt, we become active participants in our own diminishment.

And then there is the third voice. It is little wonder that we struggle in a world that constantly communicates, "As you are, you are not enough"—not enough for love, to belong, to be secure, or to matter very much at all. This not-always-subtle message can come from friend and foe, family, and even faith. So in response to the beat-down, we fight to measure up, desperately driven by the chronic belief that we must become more or else be left out of the best parts of life.

Hearing that it's all a lie doesn't seem to be enough to banish these negative thoughts. It's hard to change these self-negating messages because many of us have formed well-developed neuropathways down which such troubled thoughts constantly stream. Because this background music has been sung in our heads for so long, the music seems to be part of who we are. So we cake on the cosmetics in order to hide from ourselves and others.

The fourth voice makes me the angriest of all. The world's put-down culture has leaked into the church, and it is too often preached from the pulpit and splattered all over the pew. The community of Christ becomes victim of a harsh gospel that propagates a creed of worthlessness as the pathway to a relationship with God.

This harsh gospel is built on the belief that God's people have to recite over and again that they are low down as the condition of being lifted up. We might as well quote Marlon Brando from the motion picture *One-Eyed Jacks*, calling ourselves a "bucket of guts" in an effort to become more acceptable to God. There is little good news in that gospel. Instead of a genuine expression of the breathtaking truth of transformation that is ours in Christ, this harsh gospel leaves everyone gut-punched and sucking for air.

Am I exaggerating? I don't think so. I've struggled on and off my entire Christian life, especially when the clouds roll in. In my role of helping the broken find healing in Christ, I have spoken with thousands who wrestle with self-image problems. No one wants to admit this battle. It's just not safe to be vulnerable and honest about such things—especially in church. Judgment lurks there. It's one more place where the accusation "You don't measure up" waits to pounce.

I am not talking about weaker brothers and sisters who do not have their Christian act together but rather about people who are faithful to Jesus, Spirit-filled, and seeking to grow in their spiritual formation. They attend church regularly, give generously, and in many cases have said yes to the call of the Lord. Many are active laypeople, while others are full-time Christian workers, including pastors and missionaries.

These are good people—good people who have one significant vulnerability: they do not behold the wonder present within themselves. On an intellectual level they may confess that they are new creations in Christ, but they cannot see beyond their own brokenness to the beauty of their true selves. That leaves them wide open to the song of deception and destruction, wooing them toward the rocky shore that will break their lives apart and send them to the bottom, where despair and desolation take over.

Does background music really matter in the grand scope of life's troubles? The motion picture industry certainly thinks so. Consider all the money that's invested in order to develop just the right musical canvas upon which to tell a story. The background music to our favorite movies often engages us emotionally, sending us soaring to the heights of inspiration or causing us to dance fitfully on the edge of darkness.

The music builds in *Chariots of Fire* and I suddenly find myself running with Eric Liddell at the 1924 Summer Olympic Games, swimming for my life at the haunting sound of two simple notes that warn of disaster in *Jaws,* or lifting my arms to the crowd in celebration as I join Rudy Ruettiger being carried from the Notre Dame University football stadium in the motion picture *Rudy.*

The background music of our lives matters greatly because it sets the tone for how we will live. We must stop allowing the four-part harmony of darkness sung by the world, the devil, ourselves, and the church to form the musical canvas on which our stories unfold.

It has already taken a mighty toll. It's time to change the music. It's time to wake up to the wonder inside us.

Singing the Blues

Some might say I'm being unduly negative, singing the blues when there are other songs to be sung. They would be right at one point. I *am* being a bluesman in the truest sense of the genre. The blues combine heartbreak with celebration, pain with joy, and failure with a coming new day, all side by side. The bluesman tells the truth, and at times the truth has a painful side to it. But in the end, the blues ultimately point toward hope.

Beneath my anger at what is being robbed from God's people arises a new song of hope. That hope is not based on the naive notion that evil will soon back away from its strategy of deception, or that the world will change its tune, or that the church will entirely turn from its sad fascination with a harsher gospel. This hope is not tied to the idea that Christians will suddenly understand the miracle of their own transformation and rest securely in their divinely given identity as children of God.

Hope in the truest sense of the word comes from the belief that God himself will break through this darkness if we cry out to him. It is not in our power alone to reverse this trend toward self-judgment. Better sermons, more teachings on the true self, even books such as this one will not be enough. But if we cry out to our heavenly Father, the Holy Spirit will bring a great awakening, an awakening to the truth of who we are in Christ. He will give us eyes to see the wonder of our new nature in Christ and ears to hear the eternal song that declares that we are the masterpiece of God himself.

You see, there is another melody being sung about us that can be heard only through spiritual awakening. It is the song the Father sings over us, spoken of in Zephaniah 3. The lyrics speak of his everlasting love and of our individual worth and inestimable value. There in Zephaniah, God speaks of his longing for us and promises his care, protection, and love. He declares before heaven and earth that even previous shame will become a place of praise and honor. The Father sings of rescue, gathering, and bringing his children home to himself.

This grace-saturated melody is not only written in Zephaniah but is also spread across the pages of Scripture. In the book of Ephesians the expressions *chosen, sought after, lavished upon, protected, held firmly,* and *protected as his through the end of time* are carried by the melody of God across time, revealing how he truly feels about his children. This is how he feels about you and me, people he calls his masterpiece (Eph. 2:10 NLT).

Despite the beauty and power of God's song in Scripture, the melody is often difficult to hear when it's drowned out by all the voices declaring diminishment and desolation. Oh, we have read the words and at times even lifted our voices in church in songs of praise. Yet for many of us, the words God sings over us do not form the background music of the life we struggle to live. Brokenness seems to have calibrated our hearing to harmonize with deception, not truth. That is why we need a great awakening.

This experience of awakening will not happen through achievement, discipline, or performance. We have exhausted ourselves living to that sad tune. It will come when, like Bartimaeus, we cry out to Jesus asking him to heal our blindness, to push back the darkness so that we might see the miracle within us.

Awakened and alive in Christ, we will be able to combat the voices of darkness, not with mere concepts about our value and worth but with deep conviction about who we really are. We will have seen and touched the light of Christ inside us and will never be the same. This transformation will be far more than conceptual. It will be episodic, an experience of grace that engages our emotions and our senses and which gives us a new vision of what it means to be his children. It will begin in a moment in time but continue to grow as we are empowered by the Holy Spirit to walk with Jesus across time. By God's grace it will be an ongoing awakening, each day, each week, each month, each year as we internalize the truth of who we are in Christ, until that dark harmony of desolation no longer comes to mind.

I pray that this book will further your transformation. If so, it won't be words on a page that will awaken you. It will be a deep movement of grace.

If you invite the Holy Spirit to be present and alive as you read and as you reflect, and if you remain attentive to the deep stirrings of his presence and power, awakening will happen. With awakening may come healing, and with healing, new confidence that at the core of your being you are nothing less than the image of God himself. You will see that you have moved from a broken piece to a masterpiece. That is the wonder inside you!

EXPERIENTIAL

I encourage you to spend time positioning yourself to meet the Lord in the RING spiritual exercise. Remember the value of finding a safe, quiet place, adopting a posture of receptivity, slowing your mind and body through deep breathing, and inviting the Holy Spirit to meet you in this present moment. When you are ready, move forward to engage the Lord.

Remain in the Light

Invite in the Holy Spirit's presence as you spend time in the light of God's word to you in Zephaniah 3:14–20 (NLT):

> Sing, O daughter of Zion;
> shout aloud, O Israel!
> Be glad and rejoice with all your heart,
>   O daughter of Jerusalem!
> For the Lord will remove his hand of judgment
>   and will disperse the armies of your enemy.
> And the Lord himself, the King of Israel,
>   will live among you!
> At last your troubles will be over,
>   and you will never again fear disaster.
> On that day the announcement to Jerusalem will be,
>   "Cheer up, Zion! Don't be afraid!
> For the Lord your God is living among you.
>   He is a mighty savior.
> He will take delight in you with gladness.
>   With his love, he will calm all your fears.
>   He will rejoice over you with joyful songs."

"I will gather you who mourn for the appointed festivals;
    you will be disgraced no more.
And I will deal severely with all who have oppressed you.
    I will save the weak and helpless ones;
I will bring together
    those who were chased away.
I will give glory and fame to my former exiles,
    wherever they have been mocked and shamed.
On that day I will gather you together
    and bring you home again.
I will give you a good name, a name of distinction,
    among all the nations of the earth,
as I restore your fortunes before their very eyes.
    I, the LORD, have spoken!"

Imagine Prophetically

Give the Holy Spirit access to your imagination, allowing him to help you experience the power of his message, which includes God's song of love for you.

"The Lord has taken away your judgements, He has cast out your enemy" (Zeph. 3:15 NKJV). Allow the Spirit to help you see this happening.

"He will rejoice over you with gladness" (Zeph. 3:17 NKJV). Give the Holy Spirit permission to show you this in your imagination.

"He will quiet you with His love" (Zeph. 3:17 NKJV). Breathe in the presence of the Spirit and ask him to give you a picture of God quieting you with love.

"He will rejoice over you with singing" (Zeph. 3:17 NKJV). Allow your imagination, set apart by the Spirit, to help you encounter the wonder of this promise from your Father.

"I will appoint them for praise and fame in every land where they were put to shame" (Zeph. 3:19 NKJV). Ask the Holy Spirit to show you the ways in which your Father can give you praise in places where you had once experienced shame.

Notice

Pay attention to the awakenings that occurred as you encountered Zephaniah 3:14–20.

- What feelings arose as you realized that you are forgiven and your enemy has been cast out?
- How did realizing that God rejoices over you with gladness touch you?
- In what ways did you enter the truth that God wants to quiet you with his love?
- Did you picture God singing a song of love over you? How did that affect your understanding of God and of yourself?
- What does the truth of God's promise to turn shame into a place of praise say to you about God's love? About your value to him?
- Did you notice that not only was God singing over you, but the text begins by encouraging you to sing as well? What is the new song that you need to serve as the background music to your life?

Give Thanks

End the RING spiritual exercise with a time of thanks. What are the specific praises that arise in your heart following this time with the Lord? Write them, share them, and pray them throughout the day.

3

IMAGE-BEARER

I stared at the photograph in disbelief. I was looking at what appeared to be a great big lump of coal, about the size of the baseball I had held in my hands countless times when I was growing up. It looked like the coal my dad had dug out of the mine when he went to work every day, the same stuff my grandparents had burned in their coal furnace in the winter—just a common, easy-to-find, inexpensive, dirty old chunk of black coal.

Except for the fact that someone had just paid fifty million dollars for it! That's right. Fifty million dollars! While it looked pretty dirty and grungy from my point of view, this fist-sized rock happened to be the second largest rough diamond ever discovered. It was mined in Botswana and named the Sowelo diamond, which means "rare find" in Setswana. Rare find indeed.

I'm glad someone in Africa knew what he or she was looking at, because if it had been handed to anyone around our small town in western Pennsylvania, that semi-smooth peace of "coal" would have been chunked straight into the coal bin. Its wonder and brilliance would have been lost forever, and no one would have known the difference.

Only an expert could have seen that the rough exterior of that rock concealed something priceless. Even keener eyes as well as skilled and experienced hands would be needed to patiently and carefully free the hidden gem from its less-than-impressive outer shell. Only the surgeon-like hands of a skilled gem-cutter could have released the priceless jewel hidden deep within that dirty, black lump of coal.

Freeing a diamond from its rough exterior involves time, patience, and precise steps. First, during what's called the planning phase, a skilled lapidary must examine the rough diamond in order to determine how to cut for maximum efficiency. The process begins with the realization that every rough diamond is unique, its facets precise to the diamond's original interior makeup and design.

Next comes the cleaving, or sawing, in which the diamond is carefully separated into pieces that will become individual gems. Done correctly, something valuable emerges. After that comes the bruting, where the separate gems that emerged from the rough diamond are rounded, a process that many believe best reflects the desirability of the gem to potential buyers. Finally, the gem moves to the stage of polishing, completed by a worker known as a brillianteer, who is committed to exposing the gem's true brilliance and quality.

Brillianteer is a great word, isn't it? I'd love a brillianteer to have a go at me, polish me up until I'm a wonder to behold! I admit I wouldn't be very enthusiastic about the other stages—all the planning, cleaving, and bruting that precede. Fortunately, I'm a human being and not a rough diamond, making those stages somewhat irrelevant to real life. Or are they?

In His Image

One of the most fundamental teachings within Judeo-Christian theology is the concept of *imago Dei,* the idea that all human beings are created in the image of God. That doesn't mean God looks like us, as though he possesses human-like features. *Imago Dei* means that human beings have incredible value and worth and carry deep within the handiwork of God's creative wonder. People, regardless of age, gender, class, race, ethnicity, nation of origin, ability, disability, education, or religion, have been endowed with the breath of God's very being—made in his image and made for a purpose.

Not only do we read in Genesis that God decided to create human beings in his image (Gen. 1:26–28), both men and women alike (Gen. 5:1–3), it also states that *imago Dei* is why taking another person's life is such a horrible act (Gen. 9:6). People, all people everywhere, are image bearers, and to dishonor another is to indirectly dishonor God himself. That includes any way in which we choose to dishonor ourselves. This is fundamentally why everyone, including ourselves, deserves to be treated with dignity and respect and to receive honor as being living icons of God himself.

Reflecting upon the fact that God created and formed him, King David said that he was "fearfully and wonderfully made" (Ps. 139:14). The apostle Paul wrote, "We are God's masterpiece" (Eph. 2:10 NLT). Imagine that for a moment. You are God's work of art, fearfully and wonderfully made. Or, building from the Greek word *poeima,* which is translated "masterpiece," you are God's living poem!

If this is true, why is it so hard to believe? Maybe it's because we don't like how some people behave or because so many of them have rough exteriors. Or perhaps we don't like what we see when we look in the mirror. Image of God? You must be kidding! After all, if I'm made in the image of God, then God must be a slightly bow-legged old guy losing what gray hair he has left who has struggled for years not only with sin but also with anxiety. At least that's how I tend to misinterpret what I see in the mirror.

When we look at others in our world, we often see so much brokenness and hostility that we wonder if the writers of Scripture were either joking or got it wrong. Masterpiece, work of art, living poem? Everyone? Really? I don't see it.

Our inability to see God's image in ourselves and others speaks directly to the problem we face as humans. Sin has messed things up royally, and the hand of Satan has been all over us ever since Adam and Eve ate the apple. The evil one is determined to mar every bit of beauty God has so wonderfully created, especially the beauty in human beings.

Even the best of us bear the scars of sin and darkness, which practically smothers the flame of God's presence that abides deep within our lives. We see the mess on the surface and find it difficult to believe there is anything better deep within. In fact, many of us think that if anyone could see what was going on deep within our lives, they'd figure out that we're even worse than we look.

Nothing could be further from the truth. Jesus came in order to set us free from *everything* that is keeping the light of God's creative wonder from shining forth in us as his children. He came from heaven to bring forth the wonder God placed within us, even before the foundations of the world.

Regardless of how you feel about yourself, you are far more valuable than the Sowelo diamond. That's true even if you're more than a little rough, even if you're hearing the voices of others who are trying to diminish you. Don't believe them.

No matter our condition, we all need a master craftsman to bring out the wonder and brilliance that exists inside us. We need someone to save what is best about us. It will take time; there will most certainly be some cleaving, cutting, bruting, and polishing to come. But know this: the planning stage happened over two thousand years ago, when the Father sent Christ to make a way on the cross for every bit of our uniqueness to be restored. He has already planned for our freedom formation. And I guarantee this: there is no better brillianteer that the Holy Spirit.

Sadly, many people live and die without ever being set free, never being truly celebrated for the living poems they are, masterpieces made in the image of God.

Wonder Found and Lost

Bull Kradoc was the most reviled man in our small town. As a boy, I noticed the way men would laugh with the scent of superiority whenever they caught sight of him, pointing him out and shaking their heads in disgust. Women would cross the street if he was on the sidewalk ahead of them, and mothers would yank their kids away if they happened to stumble upon him in a doorway or alley. Bull was far from invisible in our blue-collar village, though I am sure he would have preferred it that way. Nobody wanted to be friends with a notorious town drunk.

Bull's presence along the streets of Finleyville was as much a fixture as the stores that lined Washington Avenue. He was a local character as familiar to me as Marge Lutes, who ran the post office, Ad Thomko, who cut my hair at his barbershop, and Doobie Dubbs, who handed out free wieners to kids who entered his grocery store. The name Bull Kradoc was known by everyone in town. But I doubt anyone ever knew the man himself.

Bull was in his late thirties or early forties when I became aware of him. His hair and beard were black and matted together like an old ball of twine dug up from creek-side mud. He usually smelled of alcohol and grime, collected while lying in the streets in a drunken stupor. With skin covered by a thick coat of hair, he reminded me of the gorilla suit I once saw in Rosenberg's department store at Halloween. His clothes were filthy, the evidence of too many nights sleeping in alleyways.

Even as a young boy, I knew where Bull was likely to be piled up asleep. He was predictable that way. If he wasn't lying behind the hardware store, he could be seen stumbling down Main Street, leaning in a doorway with his chin on his chest, or begging for money outside the local tavern. More than once I saw him sleeping one off behind an auto repair shop, joined at times by my Uncle Fat, who had his own problem with alcohol.

People were not kind to Bull. It wasn't just that they ignored his presence—they despised him. Teenagers were the worst. They would often steal his wine when he was sleeping, drink part of it, then urinate into the gallon jug, believing Bull deserved the abuse.

I asked some relatives how Bull ended up that way. Nobody seemed to know or care. There was a story there for sure. Maybe it was his experience as an infantry soldier in World War II, or the rotten fruit of a bad childhood, or the enduring pain of lost love. When I asked, the answer was usually, "Oh, that's just Bull. He's a drunk."

After seeing Bull stumble along for years, something happened that shocked me to the core. The Pittsburgh Pirates were going to the World Series and our town's enthusiasm had elevated to a fever pitch. Signs that read "Beat Um, Bucs" were plastered all over local stores. People were spouting off about how the Bucs were going to beat those Yankees this time. Bravado spewed from old men with big bellies and loud mouths.

In the midst of all the bragging, something happened that captured the attention of the entire town. Bull Kradoc was promised an ample supply of alcohol if he would paint murals of the Pirates on the alley walls in Finleyville. Still disheveled and unkempt, he dried out enough to create images that rivaled anything Disney had ever produced. People came from all over and stared, stupefied that this art was the work of the town drunk.

The owner of the hardware store, a guy named Orley, purchased a beat-up car and had Bull paint it bumper to bumper with images of the Pittsburgh Pirates. It was so stunning that people from big-town newspapers came and took photographs that showed up not on the sports section but on the front page. Everyone had the same reaction: "Who knew?" Certainly no one around my home thought Bull had it in him.

Sadly, Bull's light went out as soon as Bill Mazeroski hit the game-winning homer in the bottom of the ninth. Townspeople celebrated, and Bull Kradoc got lost once again in the bottle, never again to display the hidden masterpiece that shone so brightly in the fall of 1960. It seems that no one had the time or patience to help Bull find the One who had placed such wonder in him in the first place.

The Miracle of the Sea

Simon, James, and John had spent the night fishing on the Lake of Gennesaret, also known as the Sea of Galilee, before returning home exhausted and skunked. They used their last bit of energy to drag the boats to shore and work on the nets. Jesus was nearby preparing to preach the gospel of the kingdom to a crowd who had gathered. The people pressed toward him, so he turned to

Simon and asked if he would push the boat into the water a bit so he could sit there and preach.

Tired though he was, Simon may have swelled with pride that this up-and-coming rabbi had asked for his help. After Jesus finished teaching about the kingdom of God, he turned to Simon and asked him to go out fishing again.

I wonder if Simon rolled his eyes. An experienced fisherman, he would have known how hard it is to catch fish in the heat of the day. Hadn't he just spent an exhausting night on the lake with nothing to show for it? Perhaps with equal parts frustration and disbelief, Simon sighed and said yes.

When Jesus told him to let down the nets, he may have shrugged his shoulders as he complied. He knew it was an exercise in fishing futility. Yet, much to his surprise, the nets held such a large haul of fish that they started to break. Simon yelled for his partners to come quickly to help.

Simon was stunned, frightened. The sea was empty all night, and suddenly this? He fell to his knees and told Jesus to go away. Simon believed that he was nothing more than a sinful man, unworthy and unholy.

But Jesus simply said, "Don't be afraid—from now on you will fish for people!"

I wonder if Simon stared at Jesus, first in disbelief and then in hope. I imagine him thinking, "That sea was empty, and yet at the word of Jesus it gave up its treasure. I wonder if Jesus can work the miracle of the sea in me. Could Jesus bring out of me something I never even knew was there?"

We know how the story unfolds. Simon said yes to the invitation of Jesus, and in a few short years, empowered by the Holy Spirit, he was winning thousands to Christ, working miracles in the name of Jesus and helping give birth to the church—all because Jesus saw something in him that he could never see in himself.

It was a grand awakening for Simon. A smelly old fisherman transformed into the person who would build Christ's church. The change was so dramatic that Jesus gave him a new name to go along with his new awakening. He was forever after called Peter, the rock.

I am convinced that there abides in you a treasure waiting to be awakened. Somewhere deep within, hidden beneath the debris this world has cast your way, abides a treasure. It is like an uncut diamond in the rough waiting to be unearthed and set free, the God-created jewel that is your true self.

The question now is quite simple:

Will you allow the Lord to call it forth, as he did in the miracle of the sea? Will you say yes to the master craftsman, who has laid out a plan for your restoration from before time began and then set it in motion through Jesus at the cross? He placed the gems of your uniqueness there in the first place, his *imago Dei,* fearfully and wonderfully designed. The Holy Spirit, God's brillianteer, awaits to bring forth the many-faceted wonder—if only you will say yes.

EXPERIENTIAL

It's time once again to get quiet before the Lord, positioning yourself for an encounter with the One who still works miracles in the places where most only see emptiness, to find hidden gems that shine with the brilliance of his own light.

Remain in the Light

As you move into the light of God's Word, be open to the Holy Spirit revealing words, phrases, and insights that come to you in fresh ways. The reading is taken from Luke 5:1–11 (*The Message*).

Once when he was standing on the shore of Lake Gennesaret, the crowd was pushing in on him to better hear the Word of God. He noticed two boats tied up. The fishermen had just left them and were out scrubbing their nets. He climbed into the boat that was Simon's and asked him to put out a little from the shore. Sitting there, using the boat for a pulpit, he taught the crowd. When he finished teaching, he said to Simon, "Push out into deep water and let your nets out for a catch." Simon said, "Master, we've been fishing hard all night and haven't caught even a minnow. But if you say so, I'll let out the nets." It was no sooner said than done—a huge haul of fish, straining the nets past capacity. They waved to their partners in the other boat to come help them. They filled both boats, nearly swamping them with the catch. Simon Peter, when he saw it, fell to his knees before Jesus. "Master, leave. I'm a sinner and can't handle this holiness. Leave me to myself." When they pulled in that catch of fish, awe overwhelmed Simon and everyone with him. It was the same with James and John, Zebedee's sons, coworkers with Simon. Jesus said to Simon, "There is nothing to fear. From now on you'll be fishing for men and women." They pulled their boats up on the beach, left them, nets and all, and followed him.

Imagine Prophetically

You are invited to allow the Holy Spirit to take you on an imaginative journey into the story found in Luke 5:1–11. Allow the Spirit access to all your senses as you cross time to join Simon, Jesus, and the other disciples on the Lake of Gennesaret. If this practice is new to you, be patient. This is a historic way of encountering scripture, encouraged centuries ago by St. Ignatius.

Step back in time and spend the night fishing with Simon, James, and John. Sense the rocking of the boat, feel the wind on your face, smell the sea air, see the starlit sky, and touch the frustration of an empty sea.

Experience exhaustion as you help drag the boats onto the shore. Join Simon and the others as you begin to repair the nets. Sense the braided rope in your tired hands and the longing for a much-needed rest.

Watch Jesus go to Simon and ask for his help. Help Simon push the boat out onto the lake so Jesus can sit in the bow and preach. Listen to the words of the kingdom as Jesus speaks of new life and the love of God.

Feel Simon's frustration when Jesus asks to go fishing. Be willing to go with him, even in your fatigue and disbelief.

Hear Jesus say, "Let down your nets." Help pull the heavy nets up from the water, full of fish where only hours before there was nothing. Be aware that you are witnessing a miracle, and watch Simon's reaction.

Kneel before Jesus with Simon; feel the power of Christ's presence and experience the feeling of unworthiness that has swept over Simon.

Hear Jesus invite Simon to a new life, and watch as he ponders, "Could Jesus work the miracle of the sea in me?"

Watch Jesus now turn to you. What is his invitation?

Notice

Growing in awareness involves becoming alert to your senses when encountering the Word of God. Spend time, guided by the Holy Spirit, revisiting every aspect of the imaginative exercise you just engaged.

- Notice the feelings you had. Write them in your journal.
- Review what you saw, touched, smelled, tasted, and heard as you walked back in time with Jesus.
- What stirred in you spiritually? Emotionally?
- Were there deep longings that came to the surface? If so, name them.
- Do you ever feel unworthy in life? Unholy? Unwanted? Allow yourself to touch those feelings.
- What is the Lord's invitation to you? Ask him to reveal the wonder that he wants to bring to the surface of your life.

Give Thanks

I once heard a theologian say that only in thanksgiving do we become our true selves. I encourage you to take pen in hand and record your thanks. Allow a spirit of gratitude to rise up as you consider the miracle of Christ's touch upon your life and the growing awakening you are experiencing.

4

HE KNOWS YOU

My mother named me after the comic strip *Terry and the Pirates*. Terry was a young man on great adventures combating evil villains, unseemly mobsters, and the infamous pirate called "the Dragon Lady." During World War II, Terry became a fighter pilot sent on dangerous missions in the Pacific, adding to his already impressive list of exploits.

I've always been proud of my namesake and my name—well, the "Terry" part. "Wardle" is a bit hard to pronounce, kind of like saying "water" with marbles in your mouth. "Terry," though, is perfect. There were plenty of guys growing up in our little town named Bob, Dave, Gary, or Tom. There was only one Terry—me.

I was furious for an entire year of high school when Mr. Poad refused to get my name right. He would take roll and call out "Tony Woodley" instead of "Terry Wardle." I sat there in silence waiting for him to pause, look at me, smirk, and say, "Oh, there you are, Mr. Woodley." I hated his misplaced attempt at humor.

Once, a presidential candidate greeted me by name as we passed in a hotel hallway. I felt ten feet tall, especially since my family was walking with me. My son looked wide eyes at me and said, "How does he know you, Dad?" For a fleeting moment I felt like a minicelebrity. About three steps later, I realized I was wearing a name tag with "Terry" spelled out in black letters. So much for my fifteen seconds of fame.

Who Are You?

It was painful when my mother forgot my name. I knew it would come to that as she journeyed though Alzheimer's disease, but my heart broke when I became a stranger to her. Being lost to Mom at the end of her life brought to the surface a frustration that she never really knew me, especially when I was a kid. We lived in the same house seemingly ten miles apart. Mom loved and took care of me—she just didn't see me, understand my feelings, or honor my dreams.

The failure to be known during the early stages of life can stifle curiosity and thwart a child's confidence. It can lead to either an anxious overreaction to life's challenges or a hopeless numbing out that robs a child of joy. Children grow into adults who have difficulty modulating negative emotions, and while they may realize something is wrong, few are aware that their emotional difficulties are rooted in disconnection that occurred in childhood.

The path toward wholeness takes deep connection. People need to be supported and known by others in order to know themselves. If there is a person in your life who has a welcoming presence, who is curious about who you are, who is respectful of your uniqueness, who entices your individual gifting to the surface, who reacts with joyful surprise when a new dimension of your true self peeks out, you will risk becoming known. And as a result, you will better know yourself.

If, on the other hand, an important person in your world is disinterested, preoccupied, unaffirming, judgmental, rejects what they see in you, or if they have a predetermined script you must follow in order to be accepted and loved by them, you will hide and you will pretend. As a result, you will never be known, and the gift the world most needs from you could forever remain hidden from sight.

A Dog's Tale

My grandmother saw me cower when the neighbor's dog ran across the yard toward me. Later that day, she asked if I would like a dog of my own, hoping it would help me gain some confidence. Grandma knew my parents wouldn't allow it, so she promised that the dog could stay at her house and be mine to play with and name. A few days later, Grandma and Grandpap took me to my great-great uncle's farm, where his Collie had given birth to six puppies.

The mother Collie met us at the car with five of the new puppies, tails wagging and tongues licking as if I were made of chocolate ice cream. After my delightful tongue bath, I noticed that one puppy was missing. Uncle Raul said the sixth pup was hiding under the wooden porch up at the old summer house perched behind the new barn. I scurried up the hill, laid belly down in the dirt, and scooted under the dilapidated porch to see him. I had to strain my eyes in the dark shadows, but there he was, looking more like a groundhog than a Collie.

As much as my aunts and uncles tried to dissuade me, that was the dog I wanted for my own. He was as nervous as I was, hiding when it thundered, teeth chattering when big trucks drove by, and showing his teeth when anyone came close. It took time for both of us to venture out of hiding, but we become good pals. Somehow, we helped each other wrestle with fear and found a place to feel understood, safe, and wanted.

Seen, Safe, Soothed, Secure

Daniel Siegel, celebrated psychiatrist and author, uses four words to define the process of self- actualization: *seen, safe, soothed,* and *secure.* These words represent investments people must make in your life if you're to develop into the strong man or woman God intends.

Being *seen* is about far more than being noticed or recognized. It involves a long, patient, empathic gaze by a welcoming presence, communicating genuine excitement that you exist. It is the look in a person's eye saying that wonder abides in you, and that wonder will be respected and honored as it emerges from hiding. Being seen impacts how you see and define yourself, contributing to the process of self-definition, part of the journey to being known and knowing yourself.

Safe means there will be predictability and consistency in the way love and compassion are communicated to you. *Safe* is the commitment others make to protect you, to not frighten or harm you. *Safe* gives you room to fail, without judgment, and provides encouragement for you to keep on trying. It provides a framework for risk-taking, like the safety net beneath the trapeze artist at the circus. *Safe,* like *seen,* welcomes the emergence of uniqueness and wonder that abides deep within you.

There is no such thing as a problem-free life. Difficulties come, ranging from a nuisance hardly worth noticing to problems that can break body, soul, and spirit. Being *soothed* by a loving presence when that happens is essential to psychological development and resilience. A consistent and gentle connection with an empathic person encodes hope in your brain, instilling the belief that when bad things happen, help will come. Being soothed empowers you to modulate your feelings and respond rather than react. Many neuroscientists believe that being soothed, through deep relational connections in childhood, contributes to the growth and maturing of the human brain itself. It enables you to grow into adulthood better able to handle the inevitable difficulties life affords.

Being seen, safe, and soothed through deep connections with a caring person helps develop *security* in your life. Love that sees you, respects you, and helps you navigate difficulty provides a foundation for you to move into life with strength, brilliance, and wonder. It also allows you the time you need to develop and mature.

God has choreographed a unique dance for you in this life, one that best fits the specific deposit of creativity and gifting he placed within you before time began. Being seen, safe, and soothed reaches for you like an outstretched hand bidding you to step into the light and dance. When you begin to be known by others in a safe, seen, and soothed way, you will better know yourself—and what you discover about yourself in the end may take your breath away.

I Know Your Name

Your feelings may be mixed as you read this. Possibly there is gratitude as you think of all the people who invested in your awakening. It is also possible you're feeling that a journey of self-discovery is yet awaiting you. Maybe you have touched the pain of being unknown, or unseen, or you feel disappointed that your full potential has never been welcomed or released. I assure you that it's never too late. Your Father longs for you to soak in his presence where your gifting can be unleashed. He is positioned even now to take you by the hand and bring you into the light of a new awakening.

As I touched the pain of being unknown, the Holy Spirit used a single scripture to reawaken my heart to God's love and care. It happened soon after my mother entered her cloud of unknowing. Despite the fact that I had read the text countless times, the scripture spoke into the deep loneliness that was stirring within me. The Lord assured me that he knows me—by name—and is committed to my well-being and care. Isaiah 43:1–3 speaks of God creating me, forming me, ransoming me, and calling me by name. God promises to walk with me through high water and devastating fire and to save me when difficult times come my way.

As I read and reread this passage, I sensed the Lord saying, "Terry, don't be afraid. I know you, I welcome you, and I will take care of you."

God has invested deeply in our growth. Long before the concept became popular in neuroscience, the Lord was actively seeing us, keeping us safe, soothing us when difficulties came our way, and securing us, now and for all eternity. Granted, we still need human connections to call us forth. That is a given. It would serve us well, however, to understand how much God invests in our self-awakening. When we do, we can better position ourselves for the journey out of hiding.

God Sees You

One of the most celebrated scriptures in the Bible is the Aaronic blessing, found in Numbers 6:24–26. There God promises to bless you, keep you, gaze at you with love, and bring you peace. This scripture makes it crystal clear that God is *for* you. Contrary to what some may suggest, God is not angry and looking to see if you're failing him. His face lights up when he gazes upon you. His gaze is patient, empathic, and welcoming. He is excited about you and longs to call forth the wonder he so creatively placed within you before you were even born. God loves showering you with grace and, as this text suggests, turns toward you, not away from you.

God knows your longings, your dreams, your struggles, your potential, your frustrations, and your hopes. It all matters to him, and it matters to him that you know it matters. Why? Because you matter. The more you gaze at the One who is forever gazing at you, the more you will experience the peace promised in this blessing. His gift of peace leads to well-being, which is the ultimate fruit of being known and knowing yourself.

You Are Safe with God

For years, the thought of God frightened me. Religious people in my early life painted a picture of God that was terrifying. They warned of high expectations, sudden judgment, and swift punishment to follow. On the one hand, they said God was loving and wanted me to draw close, while on the other, they threatened that he was angry and capricious. For years, going to church made me nervous, similar to when I went to the dentist, only more so. It always felt better on the way out than on the way in.

If you want to know what God is really like, you need to look at Jesus (Col. 1:15; Heb. 1:3). Read the stories in the Bible about his interactions with broken people. Jesus never condemned the woman at the well for her immoral life, he greeted greedy Zacchaeus as a friend, he welcomed tax collectors and sinners into his close fellowship of followers, and he surrounded himself with broken people who needed healing and hope. They were all safe with him.

The closer you draw to God, the more you will experience his love and compassion. You are safe with God, and he has no desire to frighten you or any design to harm you. His grace makes room for you to grow and to fail. His caring arms undergird you, providing a sturdy framework for you to emerge into the fullness of your gifting and wonder. God welcomes you to step into the life he designed for you.

God Longs to Soothe You

The Lord never said you would not face difficulties in life. They are the inevitable consequence of living on the wrong side of Eden. The evil one ran rampant across the earth for generations, and every day you encounter the debris of brokenness and destruction he has left in his wake. Jesus said that you would have trouble in this world (John 16:33). Any suggestion otherwise is simply unbiblical and unfounded. His warning, however, was followed with a promise. Jesus said that he has overcome the world and that with his help you can find peace in troubled times.

Jesus promised to be with you always (Matt. 28:20). He was not suggesting that he would stand by and simply watch you stumble through life. Jesus wants to help you when things get tough (2 Cor. 12:9–10). Notice how God is described in the stories of Scripture. He has been likened to a mother hen, a refuge, a shelter, a fortress, and a rock.

Consider God's soothing love described in Psalm 23. David sings of green pastures, still waters, refreshment, and paths of righteousness. He points to God's promised rest, stillness, and restoration when things are difficult for you. The Lord sets a table for you when the going gets rough, protects and guides you with rod and staff, and is determined to chase you with overflowing abundance for the remainder of your days. These truths reflect the nature of God's love for you and are a soothing reminder that at all times and in all ways, the Lord is for you.

Your Relationship with God Is Secure

The Lord has made you an incredible promise: that nothing would separate you from his love, given to you in Christ Jesus the Lord (Rom. 8:38–39). Think about the implications of this scripture for your life. Nothing will ever disconnect you from the Lord. Nothing. You are eternally hidden in the heart of Christ. Regardless of who attacks you or how life beats down upon you, your connection with God is rock solid. You are secure on good days as well as bad, when the light is shining and when darkness threatens, as you stay nestled in his embrace and when you wander away from home. You are secure when Satan pounds on you, when powers harass you, when life seems too hard for you, and when death comes knocking at your door. You are connected with God, and God is forever connected with you, his child.

Your Father sees you, respects you, and wants to help you navigate difficulty. He welcomes your strength, your brilliance, and your wonder. His grace gives you all the time you need to develop, and he has given you his Holy Spirit to help every step along the way. If you stumble on the path, that's okay too. It's all part of learning. Allow the Lord to take your hand, and he will lead you into grand possibilities already present within your gifted life—possibilities that move you from broken to beloved.

EXPERIENTIAL

I hope reading this chapter has helped you better grasp that God is for you, welcomes you, and knows you. That is the first important step toward knowing yourself and releasing the wonder he has deposited within you. It is equally necessary that you position yourself to experience his presence. You must sense the reality of his love and care. Embracing the following spiritual exercise can position you for that awakening. I encourage you to find a safe, quiet place to meet with the Lord, settle yourself through deep breathing, and await the presence of the Holy Spirit as your helper and guide.

Remain in the Light

The following verses are God's Word. Imagine that he is gazing into your eyes and speaking directly to you. Ask the Holy Spirit to help you receive his promise into your heart as a gift of love. Move slowly and carefully as you read.

> You who sit down in the High God's presence,
>   spend the night in Shaddai's shadow,
> Say this: "GOD, you're my refuge.
>   I trust in you and I'm safe!"
> That's right—he rescues you from hidden traps,
>   shields you from deadly hazards.
> His huge outstretched arms protect you—
>   under them you're perfectly safe;
>   his arms fend off all harm.
> Fear nothing—not wild wolves in the night,
>   not flying arrows in the day,
> Not disease that prowls through the darkness,
>   not disaster that erupts at high noon.
> Even though others succumb all around,
>   drop like flies right and left,
>   no harm will even graze you.
> You'll stand untouched, watch it all from a distance,

watch the wicked turn into corpses.
Yes, because GOD's your refuge,
 the High God your very own home,
Evil can't get close to you,
 harm can't get through the door.
He ordered his angels
 to guard you wherever you go.
If you stumble, they'll catch you;
 their job is to keep you from falling.
You'll walk unharmed among lions and snakes,
 and kick young lions and serpents from the path.

"If you'll hold on to me for dear life," says GOD,
 "I'll get you out of any trouble.
I'll give you the best of care
 if you'll only get to know and trust me.
Call me and I'll answer, be at your side in bad times;
 I'll rescue you, then throw you a party.
I'll give you a long life,
 give you a long drink of salvation!"
 (Ps. 91 *The Message*)

Imagine Prophetically

Invite the Holy Spirit to take over your imagination, using it to communicate through your mind and senses. Spend time with specific images in these texts, inviting the Spirit to help you "see" and experience what each is communicating about God's love and commitment to you.

Spend time imagining the Lord blessing you. See him draw close with his arms filled with gifts designed just for you.

Ask the Holy Spirit to unfold each of the following images:

- God keeping you
- God's face shining as he gazes at you
- God pouring grace lavishly upon you
- God turning toward you, and never away
- You at peace in God's arms

Psalm 91 is full of descriptive images of God's care for you. Focus on one of the following and allow the Holy Spirit to bring it to life. Stay present to all your senses as you do.

- Sitting in God's presence
- Resting in Shaddai's shadow
- God as your refuge
- Safe
- Secure in his outstretched arms
- God as your home
- Taking "a long drink of salvation"

Notice

Having completed the above, be attentive to your feelings. Notice what is going on emotionally as you consider the love and care God is extending to you.

Notice your level of body tension. What is your body trying to tell you?

Which of the images above most capture your imagination?

What affect will these truths have on your willingness to take the Father's hand?

What feelings are you experiencing as you consider the reality of wonder being present within your life?

What practical steps will you take to soak more deeply in the promises of God's love and care?

Give Thanks

Spend time writing a brief psalm of thanksgiving. Use the following from Psalm 9 as a guide.

I will give thanks to you, LORD, with all my heart;
    I will tell of all your wonderful deeds.
I will be glad and rejoice in you;
    I will sing the praises of your name, O Most High.
    (Ps. 9:1–2)

5

WELCOMING THE
WEAKEST PART OF YOU

His worst nightmare was little more than a childish fantasy compared to the debilitating darkness that had descended upon him. Weakness, long hidden beneath layers of defense, overtook him with the force of an emotional tsunami. In what seemed like an instant, life as he knew it changed forever. So had people's opinion of him as a Christian leader.

He had invested heavily in his career and advanced beyond his peers. He had earned his doctorate, became the head of a theological seminary at the age of thirty-three, an author a year later, then a successful pastor and a sought-after public speaker.

He had also started one of the fastest growing churches in his denomination, which brought him much-needed recognition among his coworkers and friends. Success brought with it satisfaction, something he had pursued his entire life. Visions that took shape when he first received the "call" to ministry began unfolding before his eyes. However, what he refused to see ended up breaking him.

Little about his childhood would have predicated the path he would take in life. His father, following his own father and grandfather, never finished elementary school. His family distrusted people with "book learning," considering them soft. It was the men with dirt under their fingernails and faces red from the sun whom they respected. Sweat was like cologne to them; worn-out work clothes the only suit of armor worthy of a real man.

The men in his blue-collar family had a disdain for religious types. Tools and guns fit comfortably in their hands, not Bibles and church bulletins. Religion was about rules, and rules were followed only when convenient.

Older men swapped tales of fast cars, big bucks, and sexual exploits, told to younger boys like history lessons, with hopes that they would someday add their stories to the family narrative. Bible verses were reserved for old women teaching little children in Sunday School.

As a teenager, he was desperate to be accepted by the company of men, so he followed their lead. Anger and rebellion grew, but anxiety and fear chased him like a fire-breathing dragon. Childhood trauma and abuse left ugly wounds that refused to be silent.

One day, while on an ever-troubling path, the Lord laid claim to his life. The experience of divine presence was undeniable. While change did not come easily, grace won out over time. He decided to follow Jesus and was determined to focus all the energy he gave to being "a real man" to living for God. Over time, he proved his commitment to the Lord and to his peers. He was accomplished, he was recognized, and he had finally become a somebody.

Then the storm hit with hurricane force. At the very time when he might have celebrated a job well done, the unhealed wounds of the past caught up to him, and what followed was a season of heartbreaking and, to many, embarrassing brokenness.

He secretly entered a psychiatric hospital for treatment. His image was shattered. Instead of being praised for his accomplishments, he was forever identified with his brokenness, his weakness, and his fall from grace. He entered a long dark night that fueled unbelief. His dreams died before hope could be born.

Over time, God's light broke through the clouds of depression and fear, but not as the reward of faith, for there was little left. It was a grace awakening. God touched the wounds that had broken him, the places that others now believed disqualified him. There, in the weakest place of his life, God showed his strength. There, in the worst part of his story, a deeper relationship with the Lord took root.

Today, he speaks of how broken pieces become *master*pieces when grace rushes in. The large church, the seminary leadership, rubbing shoulders with the celebrated and praised are long past. He has become forever linked to the weak part of his story, the fragile part of his story, the broken place in his story—now the best part of his story. He walks with the bruised and the beat-up, pointing them to the One who does his best work in weak and wounded places.

He is not sure why Jesus pays so much attention to weakness or how grace flows best through the broken places, though he knows it does. It is all a paradox, why strength and weakness go together so well. But he knows they do, and he talks about it to as many people as he can. I know this story well—for it is mine.

Chaos and Cosmetics

Many of us go to great lengths to hide imperfections and weaknesses, and for good reason. Most people live in societal subcultures that are quick to judge. Folks are held at arm's length when they do not measure up to the standards of acceptance others deem appropriate. Ridicule comes swiftly and severely at times, relegating undesirables to the cheap seats where, if they strain, they can watch the perfect people experience the good life.

Weakness and imperfection are like blood in the water. Once the sharks catch the scent, things go bad quickly. That seems especially true for those of us who have battled emotional weaknesses. People are not always gracious or understanding when people struggle with psychological problems. The unschooled and unaware seem to think problems like anxiety, depression, obsessive behaviors, and the like are simply the result of "stinkin' thinkin'," so they coldly advise, "Get over it."

In response, we hide and cover up. And why not? I spent years hiding my struggle with anxiety from other people and from myself as well. The fear was bad enough, but when ridicule came for being the "nervous" type, I felt alone in a struggle against an unseen monster determined to devour me.

I hauled a truck load of shame and embarrassment around as a result. Over time, I grew to hate the little guy inside, that wimpy, much-afraid character. I wished him dead or forever condemned to an isolated island where I would never feel his pain again. Sadly, self-hatred birthed more fear, which eventually spilled over in adulthood, demanding a long season of intense care.

Our society is not all that kind to people who have physical imperfections either. In fact, it can be brutal. My family zeroed in on a person's perceived physical imperfection and made it the centerpiece of their identity. My great-uncle George was forever known in the family as "Hook" because of the eagle-like shape of his huge nose. My grandmother's brother Fred was called "Uncle Fat" because of the mountain of flesh that spilled over his belt.

In a "You don't measure up" culture, physical struggles, especially those that are not easily covered by cosmetics or corrected through surgery, become a daily reminder of why some people are relegated to the cheap seats.

My heart broke as I listened to a tragic story from one of my doctoral students. We were discussing emotional wounding caused by people's reaction to others' physical imperfections, and he began to weep.

"Do you know what it's like knowing, every day of your life, that you're the ugliest baby your mother ever saw?" He said those were the first words his mother said when she saw him after his birth. This dear, successful, fifty-year-old man told us that damning statement welcomes him every day whenever looks in the mirror.

Thousands of people have felt dismissed and disenfranchised because of what others believe to be unacceptable. Weaknesses and perceived imperfections can cause people to feel unfairly cursed by a God "the beautiful people" call *loving*.

Then, of course, there is the question of sin. We all fall into that ditch, which is why we so badly need Jesus. But the church community can be a judgmental lot. We fear that God's people will react harshly to our stories of wandering, whether past or present. So we hide, often at a time when we should be calling out for help.

I remember well the day my seminary professor warned us never to be open about our own struggles. He told us that doing so would quickly disqualify us from ministry. That was the day I realized that serving God was not just about declaring the perfection of Christ but also about meeting the demand for my own perfection as well. The problem is that I and many others are prone to wander. I'm not excusing such behavior, but it's true and inevitable in this broken world.

Jesus has taken care of my wandering and has washed, covered, and forever cast aside my sin. But experience tells me that "good Christians" can respond to moral weakness with a holier-than-thou gasp. I'm sure I've blown out a bit of hot air myself when someone chose to be honest about a particular vulnerability.

Is it really a surprise, then, that many of us construct walls for self-protection? No one wants to feel the sting of rejection or judgment. There are good reasons we relegate weaknesses to the dark, damp basement of our lives. Unfortunately, weakness tends to grow in those dark recesses of the soul.

God has another plan for brokenness and imperfection. As hard as it may be to believe, he does some of his best work in the very places we would rather hide.

Boast in Weakness?

The apostle Paul once wrote that he had come to boast in his weaknesses, even delight in them (2 Cor. 12: 9–10). Boast in weaknesses? Delight in weaknesses? Who does that? Why do that? Isn't it an invitation to experience rejection or ridicule? Like so many of the teachings of Christ, this upside-down approach is actually the pathway to freedom and intimacy with God.

Paul struggled with significant pain and embarrassment. He never shared the specifics, but over the centuries a whole lot of people have tried to guess his problem. Whatever it was, or however it happened, this weakness was a serious matter for Paul. He called it "a thorn in my flesh" and "a messenger of Satan" (2 Cor. 12:7).

Paul prayed hard for God to remove this "thorn." I have done the same about my struggle with anxiety. When Paul wrote that he "pleaded" with the Lord to take it away, I could relate. Been there, done that!

Jesus spoke to Paul, and what he said transformed Paul's perspective on weakness. Christ said, "My grace is sufficient for you, for my power is made perfect in weakness" (2 Cor. 12:9). The Lord promised to fill Paul with power in the very place that Paul was so desperate to eliminate from his life. Instead of it being a liability, with the touch of Jesus, weakness became an asset to Paul's life and ministry.

Paul stopped begging Jesus to take the weakness away and started bragging about it. "I delight in weaknesses, in insults, in hardships, in persecutions, in difficulties. For when I am weak, then I am strong" (2 Cor. 12:10.) Paul understood that weakness was a way to encounter the strength of the Lord.

Meeting Jesus in Weaknesses

What does it mean to meet Jesus in your weakness? Let's start with what it does *not* mean. The Lord doesn't want you to pretend that everything is okay or hide the fact that you have struggled. Meeting Jesus in your weakness doesn't mean you have to haul it out in front of everyone, especially around people who might poke you in the eye over it. You also don't have to keep your mouth shut about your weakness—not with the Lord. Jesus doesn't mind when you beg him to take the weakness or imperfection away.

Meeting the Lord in weakness *does* mean that, after all the prayers and pleading, you are willing to allow the Lord to meet you in the struggle. At times that means experiencing the Lord's grace and strength in the midst of your pain, even when the problem does not quickly go away, possibly never goes away.

I spent years asking the Lord to heal my anxiety. It didn't go away or get better for a long, long time. I did, however, experience his compassionate presence as I cried out, and Jesus helped me hold on when I didn't think I could take one more minute of the pain. Admittedly, I was frustrated that my anxiety didn't suddenly disappear, but I grew to experience Jesus there with me. Over time, I noticed that my intimacy with Jesus was growing as I cried out to him.

There came a time when the gift of his presence in the midst of my struggle became more precious than my desire for freedom. The very thing Satan was using to break me, anxiety, became the weakness the Lord used to draw me more deeply into his embrace, when at my best I even began giving thanks for the struggle.

There are times when meeting Jesus in weakness means allowing him to use that weakness or imperfection as a place of ministry to help other people. That's what the Lord has done with my journey toward emotional wholeness. Many people told me to hide the fact that I had spent time in a psychiatric hospital. One Christian leader actually warned me that sharing my story would cost me my ministry.

Well, maybe he was right. In a way I did lose *my* ministry and have spent my life since the breakdown doing *his* ministry. I get to help the broken, the beat up, and the bruised. What Satan tried to use to destroy me has become the broken place where Christ's light shines out to help others. This is one of the most amazing aspects of God's love and grace. The weakness you try hardest to hide can become, by grace, the very place where you experience your most impactful ministry.

Charles Colson went to prison for participating in the Watergate scandal, met Jesus, and ended up spending the rest of his life caring for men and women who were incarcerated. Joni Eareckson Tada had a swimming accident at the age of seventeen that left her paralyzed and has since spent her life caring for thousands of people with disabilities. Author Philip Yancey has been frank about his struggles with doubt, yet has written books that have helped tens of thousands hold on when life hurts.

The names of people God has used like this could go on and on. Some are well known, but most are everyday Christians who have found that Jesus was right: grace is a powerful gift, and no matter how weak we may be, the Lord can pour his strength right through the broken places when we offer them to the Lord.

Now comes the more difficult question. What if your weakness is not emotional or physical—but moral? What if a particular sin has you by the throat? How does Paul's teaching about boasting and delighting in weakness relate to that?

Make no mistake: God's grace is lavish, scandalous, and at times hard to describe. You catch a glimpse of this grace in Bible stories about Jesus, like his encounter with the woman at the well, the Gadarene demoniac, Zacchaeus, the woman caught in adultery, and the apostle Paul on the Road to Damascus. Each one of these people struggled with weakness. While many would have scorned them for their brokenness, Jesus drew them into his embrace.

There is no judgment hidden within the grace Christ extends to you, nor does he condemn you because of weakness. The Lord draws close even when there is sin, and he comes with empathy and compassion. He never rejects you, nor does he abandon you.

Jesus does not turn a blind eye toward moral struggles. He addresses them head on by looking beyond our sin to the true weakness that gives birth to our bad behavior. Ignatius once said that Satan attacks us at our weakness. Most people would say that the particular sin we engage in is our weakness. Ignatius disagrees. Our weakness is the unmet longing that lies beneath those sinful actions.

Let's imagine for a moment that there is a man named Bill who struggles with a sexual addiction. Clearly that is sin. But that sinful desire is not his weakness. His weakness may be that he longs for love, or belonging, or significance, and can't find it. The pain of that unmet longing, his weakness, becomes too much for Bill. In comes the evil one who tempts Bill to kill the pain brought on by his unmet longing, weakness, through sexual addiction.

This is where Paul's words really come to play. Bill needs to go beyond praying that the Lord will take away his sexual misconduct. Bill needs the grace of Christ to flow into the weakness that drives that problem in the first place. He needs Jesus to touch his unmet longing, whether it be the desire for love, or acceptance, or significance. Bill's sexual addiction is a symptom of a much deeper problem—a problem that the Lord's strength is powerful enough to meet head on.

Bill needs to turn to the Lord in repentance. Many people identify repentance as a season of great sorrow in which a person finally admits he or she has blown it, needs help, and grovels his or her way back to God. Biblical repentance is far more positive, like entering home after a long, hard day. In his book *The Indwelling Life of Christ,* Major W. Ian Thomas wrote,

> True repentance is not being sorry for something you
> have done wrong. No, if you do something wrong
> you should be sorry; but that is not repentance. . . .
> Real repentance is hilariously exciting. It is facing the
> facts, recognizing how God made you, how you were
> intended to function, and then being restored to that
> relationship of mutual interavailability that the Lord
> enjoyed between Himself and the Father.[1]

So can the Lord use people who struggle with moral weakness? Of course—once we allow him to meet us at the unmet core longing that drives our sin in the first place. That is where the Lord's strength and grace are at their transforming best. Please make no mistake: the world needs to hear from men and women who meet Jesus in the very places that others have judged and rejected.

Jesus Christ offers you the same promise he gave to Paul. "My grace is sufficient for you, for my strength is made perfect in weakness" (2 Cor. 12:9). Welcome the weakest part, whether it is psychological, physical, even moral. Recognize that within the weakness is a hidden gift from God. Place your arm around that weak part of yourself, and then gently and patiently walk together toward Jesus, meeting him in a way you never dreamed possible. Soon you too will say, "I will boast in my weaknesses, for when I am weak, he is strong."

EXPERIENTIAL

I encourage you once again to engage the RING spiritual exercise. It would be easy to simply move on to the next chapter. Please don't. Go to your sacred space, quiet your heart and mind, and make room for the Lord's presence. The Holy Spirit, your great helper, is positioned to draw you into his embrace, willing to empower this moment in time. He offers you an experience that will draw you into a deeper spiritual awakening.

Remain in the Light

The Scripture reading is taken from 2 Corinthians 12:7–10. I have chosen to use *The Message* because it provides special insight into the relationship between weakness and the grace of Jesus Christ. The choice of words and images used by Eugene Peterson are not only enriching but will also help make the Word of God come alive in your heart and mind. Remember: ask the Holy Spirit to help you engage the text.

Because of the extravagance of those revelations, and so I wouldn't get a big head, I was given the gift of a handicap to keep me in constant touch with my limitations. Satan's angel did his best to get me down; what he in fact did was push me to my knees. No danger then of walking around high and mighty! At first I didn't think of it as a gift, and begged God to remove it. Three times I did that, and then he told me,

My grace is enough; it's all you need.

My strength comes into its own in your weakness. Once I heard that, I was glad to let it happen. I quit focusing on the handicap and began appreciating the gift. It was a case of Christ's strength moving in on my weakness. Now I take limitations in stride, and with good cheer, these limitations that cut me down to size—abuse, accidents, opposition, bad breaks. I just let Christ take over! And so the weaker I get, the stronger I become. (2 Cor. 12:7–10 *The Message*)

Imagine Prophetically

Invite the Holy Spirit to use your imagination to help you better experience the power of God's Word. Engage the Scripture personally, moving beyond reading verses to an encounter with God around your weaknesses and pain.

- What does it mean to you that Paul writes of "the gift of a handicap"? How can a handicap be a gift? Did the Lord bring to mind a specific struggle? If so, what was it?

- Ask the Spirit to help you see ways in which Satan has tried to get you down because of your struggles. What has that struggle with darkness cost you?
- As your read of Paul's pleading for relief, touch your own cries to God for healing and deliverance. Hear your own cries for help.
- Invite the Holy Spirit to help you see Jesus standing before you, with arms outstretched. What does he say to you about your struggle? Ask him what "my grace is sufficient" means for you.
- Allow yourself permission to imagine the Lord's power flowing into your weakness.
- Are you able to give the Lord permission to flow through your weakness to help others? If so, step out and make that offer. If not, talk to him about why.

Notice

Spend a few moments doing a body scan, concentrating on each part of your body, moving slowly from your head all the way down to your toes. What do you notice about the tension level in your body while doing this exercise?

- What feelings arose in you when you contemplated the phrase, "the gift of a handicap?"
- How did you react when considering how Satan tries to use your weaknesses to bring discouragement and unbelief? What did you sense going on inside?
- As you touched your own prayers for help and deliverance, what feelings arose?

- What did you experience as you encountered Jesus standing before you offering grace and strength?

Feel free to begin a conversation with Jesus about the frustrations of your lingering weaknesses, and the hope that they will actually draw you closer to him.

Give Thanks

Gratitude is a spiritual discipline. It does more than provide space for you to say thanks to the Lord for his presence. It invites more of his light into your life and seals within your heart the work the Lord is doing. Gratitude is also a proven weapon against the forces of darkness. Take time to write your thanks, pray your thanks, and share what you may have learned and received from the Lord through this exercise.

NOTE

[1] Major W. Ian Thomas, *The Indwelling Life of Christ: All of Him in All of Me* (Colorado Springs: Multnomah Books, 2006), 103.

6

FEASTING
AT HIS TABLE

Two days each week stood out above the rest when I was a boy: Monday and Thursday—or, as I referred to them, "washday" and "hotdog day." One day was filled with tension as my sister and I tried to meet our mother's expectations, or at least not make her angry. The other day was marked by the gentle touch of church ladies wearing hand-sewn aprons and disposable serving gloves. One day put my stomach in knots. The other gave me room to breathe. One day was as unpleasant as enemas and castor oil. The other was a calm repose from an otherwise crazy life.

Unresolved grief can manifest in a person's life in many ways, none of them good. For my mother, who experienced several tragedies as a child, loss led to a series of compulsive behaviors, not the least of which was keeping everything in her world, both animate and inanimate, clean. She scrubbed floors, walls, pots, pans, appliances, and toilets as though she were fighting the devil himself.

Every Monday, like clockwork, my mother awakened us with the reminder that it was washday. Before and after school we had specific duties to be carried out with precision. The regimen Mom oversaw would rival any wartime military operation.

Dirty socks had to be rubbed with fels naphtha soap, scrubbed against the washboard, before being thrown into the washing machine. Clothes were stacked in piles around the washer according to fabric and color. They were placed in the washing machine in a specific order, run through the ringer twice, hung on the line to dry, folded, and then moved to the table next to the ironing board. Everything but socks and sheets was ironed, including underwear, T-shirts, handkerchiefs, and pillowcases. There was exactness to these tasks, and mistakes were not tolerated.

There's nothing wrong with being clean. It just shouldn't be a quasi-religious ritual monitored with threats of hellfire. Maybe cleanliness is next to godliness, but in our home, cleanliness *was* godliness, and washday was supervised with "naughty or nice" watchfulness.

"Hotdog day" was different. I attended a small elementary school nestled close to the railroad tracks at the bottom of our steep hill. Most kids walked to school and carried lunches in either brown paper bags or lunch boxes. There wasn't a cafeteria, so when the noon bell rang, we sat at our desks and ate quietly—that is, except for Thursdays.

The elementary school shared a small parking lot with the church next door. To raise funds, ladies from the congregation would prepare hotdogs to sell to kids who attended my school.

Grade by grade, kids were lined up in the school hallway, then quietly walked single file across the lot and into the side door of the church. We descended the steps and paid our dollar to the church lady at the corner table. We then passed in front of the kitchen, where church ladies, wearing cotton dresses, aprons, and disposable gloves, gave us our lunches. We were handed a flimsy white cardboard box containing two hotdogs, a bag of chips or pretzels, and a can of pop (otherwise known as soda).

I loved hotdog day. Every Thursday morning, I sat at my desk fingering the dollar bill in my hand, waiting for the bell to ring. I could escape the classroom for a while, since my teacher didn't make the holy descent into the church basement. I ate hotdogs, chips, and soda for lunch, instead of my usual dry sandwich, warm milk from a cheap thermos, and a stale graham cracker covered with icing. I was allowed to sit at whatever table I wanted, laugh, talk with friends, and eat without anyone complaining about my manners.

I loved the church ladies. They called me by name, smiled, and often give me a big hug. A couple of the church ladies were great-aunts who made a fuss when I walked through the line. I felt special, I belonged, I was protected.

For one hour every Thursday, in a simple concrete basement in the church next to the elementary school, I experienced rest from my otherwise crazy-making anxiety. The world was a better place when I had a hotdog in my hand. It still is.

"Washing" or "Feasting"?

How would you describe the Christian life? "Washday" or "hotdog day"? I assure you that is not a silly question. Your answer might reveal your understanding of the gospel as well as what it means to be a child of God.

A lot of people have a "washday" perspective of the Christian life. Many, myself included, have been taught that God insists that we clean up our act or else. We're warned that God watches to see how we're behaving, so we must be careful. Granted, he is willing to forgive our sins when we come to faith in Christ, but afterward, we need to pay special attention to rules and rituals. If we do, blessings will follow. When we do not, the wrath of God hangs over our heads like the sword of Damocles.

"Washday" is a transactional understanding of the Christian life. *Do* good, *get* good. Do *bad* . . . well, you get it. It is founded on the belief that the blessings of God are distributed in direct proportion to a person's practice of practical holiness. God doesn't like your kind of dirt and insists that regular washdays are the only solution. Clean people are acceptable people, so you had better follow the cosmic instructions for wash, rinse, and repeat.

At the heart of "washday" theology is the presupposition that security with God is conditioned upon clean living. Christians who promote this theology are quick to provide a list of what "real Christians" do and don't do, hoping that you will work hard proving you are the real deal.

"Washday" theology is exhausting. It's also the breeding ground for the conflicting emotions of pride and anxiety. We puff our chests thinking we have earned our blessings, or we become anxious about our behavior, hoping to keep God's anger at bay. There is zero rest in "washday" theology because there may be hell to pay if we fail to scrub hard enough. No matter what we did with today's dirt, tomorrow will start the entire wash cycle over again.

To be clear, sin matters. There is a later chapter that takes up that topic directly. But the idea that personal efforts at cleansing provide the basis of security and acceptance from God is wrong headed. It prioritizes human behavior over the scandalous grace provided for us through faith in Christ.

Imagine a great feast set before you. It is lavish and extravagant beyond your wildest dreams. The food is capable of satisfying your deepest longings and fulfilling your wildest dreams. It is a table set by God, laid out specifically for you, able to satisfy your need for love, acceptance, safety, security, and significance.

There's one catch, though. What if permission to sit and eat is based upon how well you follow the rules? Or, using the concept of washday, what if you get to eat only when you have worked hard scrubbing away the day's dirt? Being nourished would rest upon the quality of your sin management for that day. Even if you had a particularly good day fighting sin, you would have no guarantee about tomorrow. While you may experience some satisfaction for a job well done today, you would be anxious wondering if you would be clean enough to sit at his table again tomorrow.

I find "washday" theology unbiblical and a barrier to joy. The table of the Lord is actually a place of acceptance, abundance, embrace, and freedom. It is open to you even when you come covered in dirt and grime. The table of the Lord is "hotdog day" on steroids, with more love and affection than even the best church ladies could provide. Jesus paid for your seat, and because you have placed your faith in him, you get to eat until your heart is content. Instead of happening only on Thursdays, the table of the Lord is set before you every day of your life.

Feasting with Jesus

Jesus loved eating with people and telling stories about great parties. One day, he was at a banquet where he saw people fighting for places of honor near the host. Jesus told the guests that humility was far more attractive in the kingdom than trying to look important in front of other people. (Luke 14:11). He encouraged them to welcome the disfranchised to their tables, like the handicapped, poor, and blind (Luke 14:13).

It appears the guests weren't all that moved by what Jesus said, so he told them a parable about a great feast. He said there once was a banquet where the invited guests acted snooty about coming on time, so the host went out and found common folk and welcomed them at his table (Luke 14:16–23). Hoping to shock his listeners out of religious pride, Jesus pointed to how God welcomes even those whom others find unworthy. He wanted them to see that God's arms were wide open to all his children, even the dirty, unwashed ones.

On another occasion Jesus met a tax collector named Levi and invited him to become one of his followers. Levi was so moved that he held a party, inviting a crowd of his tax collector pals to share an evening with Jesus. This bothered the religious leaders, and they asked Jesus why he ate with tax collectors and sinners. Jesus simply said that it was the sinners who needed him (Luke 5:27–32). The leaders were so angry at this response and so offended that Jesus would associate with undesirables that they threatened to kill him.

Those religious leaders were in bondage to "washday" theology. They insisted that only rule-keepers get to eat at the table of the Lord. Jesus could not be from God if he spent time enjoying the embrace of the high-smelling and low-down. So they called Jesus a "glutton and a drunkard, a friend of tax collectors and sinners" believing it to be the height of insult (Matt. 11:19). Jesus took it as a compliment.

You may be concerned that I am perhaps promoting a cheap form of grace. Before you do that, please keep reading. I think you'll find that it's actually the opposite. Grace comes at a high price and only Jesus could pay it. It cost Jesus everything to embrace us into his forever family.

Jesus told another story about a feast in Luke 15. It is the most famous parable of Jesus, one of the greatest stories of all time. The setting for the story is a large farm in ancient Palestine.

It begins with a young son who was frustrated with life on the farm and demanded that his father give him a bundle of cash and his freedom. This would have been a huge insult to the father, shaming him in the eyes of his family, friends, and employees. To ask for an inheritance before your father was dead was the same as *wishing* him dead. Instead of reacting to his son's brutally selfish request, the father, who was full of grace, provided the inheritance and watched his boy walk away from everything that was right and good.

The son traveled to a distant country, and free from restraint, he went on a spending spree, engaging in behaviors that were ill advised and immoral. He jumped into the dirt with both feet, and before he knew it, he was neck deep in pig mud, eating any vile thing he could get his hands on.

Every day the father looked down the long road, watching to see if his son was coming home. The distance of time and space had only increased the father's desire to surround his son with care and protection. Rebellion could not diminish the power of his love.

A great famine finally broke the son, and, famished, he devised a scheme that might satisfy his hunger. He would go home, and if his father received him, he would lay down a sob story about sorrow and repentance, hoping that "Ol' Dad" would break and allow him back on the farm. He would say, "I'm not worthy to be called your son anymore—just hire me as one of your lowly farm hands." Maybe a performance like that would get him a decent meal and a place to sleep.

One day as the father was once again gazing down the road, he saw his son limping home. The father hiked up his robe and took off running. Hired hands watched in stunned silence as the father, the one offended, humbled himself to take off at a sprint after a wayward and, in their eyes, undeserving child. He grabbed his son, threw his arms around him, and kissed him. That dirty, smelly, wandering son was in his arms again and that was all that mattered to the father.

Everyone was stunned. The wealthy father didn't bring up the way the son had hurt him. He didn't tell him to clean up or prove himself. The father just shouted for the party to begin! The fatted calf was turned into a sumptuous feast, a celebration of a father's love for his lost child, alive in his arms once again. A new robe was placed on the son, even before he had scrubbed off the filth. He was given a special ring, the symbol of authority and honor, given freely to one who had abused the privilege.

Why was the father so forgiving? Because that young man had always been his beloved child. He was the son when he was growing up safe at home, the son when he offended his father, the son when he wandered away, the son when he was covered in filth, and the son when he halfheartedly returned to the family farm. Nothing, including his dirt, ever compromised his standing with his father nor his place at the table. Why? Because his seat was secured through sonship, through relationship, and not because he returned home clean.

This is a story about the lavishness of God's love. Jesus told this parable so you would know that eating at the table of the Lord is not based on behavior or cleaning up your act. Your seat at the table of the Lord is secure because you are his child, through faith in Christ. As 1 John 3:1 says, "See how very much our Father loves us, for he calls us his children, and that is what we are!" (NLT). How much does the Father love you? He calls you his child, and that is precisely who you are!

The table of the Lord is spread before you today. Your deepest desires can be filled there: love, acceptance, security, significant, purpose, and understanding. You are free to eat and drink all you want. Like noted in Psalm 23, the Lord sets the table before you, right in the presence of your worst enemies. He anoints you at his table, your cup overflows at his table, and goodness and mercy will chase you every day for the rest of your life (Ps. 23:6). Why? Because you've always loved him well and done the right thing? No, simply because you are his child.

The parable of the son includes one more scene. The father had another son who wasn't happy about his father's generosity toward his younger brother. He believed his brother deserved to be punished, or at the very least disciplined for a long season, before he could sit again at the father's table. The younger son came home a dirty mess, and his brother believed cleansing was the prerequisite to acceptance. In his mind, his younger brother had to prove he would work hard at sin management.

People who buy into "washday" theology often feel the same way about the beat-up, bruised, and broken. They don't understand the scandalous grace of God that allows you to sit at the table of the Lord simply because you are his child.

You are the Father's child and there is nothing you need to add, nothing to earn. While it can be difficult when some of your brothers and sisters insist that you clean up, just love them—don't listen to them. Your seat is secure. At the table of the Lord, your behavior just doesn't matter. Jesus Christ has given you a seat, simply because you trust in him.

I guess it would be trite calling this "hotdog day" theology. I have to admit, though: it works for me!

EXPERIENTIAL

Don't underestimate the importance of positioning yourself in order to best experience these spiritual exercises. In some ways, positioning is more important than the exercise itself. There is something powerful about finding a safe, quiet place where you can meet the Lord. Several deep breaths will help focus your mind and body, raising your awareness to the gentle wind of the Spirit's presence.

Remain in the Light

I invite you to slowly meditate on the story of the prodigal son. Ask the Holy Spirit to help you hear Jesus telling it, as though he were speaking directly to you.

A man had two sons. When the younger told his father, "I want my share of your estate now, instead of waiting until you die!" his father agreed to divide his wealth between his sons.

A few days later this younger son packed all his belongings and took a trip to a distant land, and there wasted all his money on parties and prostitutes. About the time his money was gone a great famine swept over the land, and he began to starve. He persuaded a local farmer to hire him to feed his pigs. The boy became so hungry that even the pods he was feeding the swine looked good to him. And no one gave him anything.

When he finally came to his senses, he said to himself, "At home even the hired men have food enough and to spare, and here I am, dying of hunger! I will go home to my father and say, 'Father, I have sinned against both heaven and you, and am no longer worthy of being called your son. Please take me on as a hired man.'"

So he returned home to his father. And while he was still a long distance away, his father saw him coming, and was filled with loving pity and ran and embraced him and kissed him.

His son said to him, "Father, I have sinned against heaven and you, and am not worthy of being called your son—"

But his father said to the slaves, "Quick! Bring the finest robe in the house and put it on him. And a jeweled ring for his finger; and shoes! And kill the calf we have in the fattening pen. We must celebrate with a feast, for this son of mine was dead and has returned to life. He was lost and is found." So the party began.

Meanwhile, the older son was in the fields working; when he returned home, he heard dance music coming from the house, and he asked one of the servants what was going on.

"Your brother is back," he was told, "and your father has killed the calf we were fattening and has prepared a great feast to celebrate his coming home again unharmed."

The older brother was angry and wouldn't go in. His father came out and begged him, but he replied, "All these years I've worked hard for you and never once refused to do a single thing you told me to; and in all that time you never gave me even one young goat for a feast with my friends. Yet when this son of yours comes back after spending your money on prostitutes, you celebrate by killing the finest calf we have on the place."

"Look, dear son," his father said to him, "you and I are very close, and everything I have is yours. But it is right to celebrate. For he is your brother; and he was dead and has come back to life! He was lost and is found!" (Luke 15:11–32 TLB)

Imagine Prophetically

- Invite the Holy Spirit to take over your imagination so that you may better enter this story.
- Imagine that you are one of the hired hands who overhears the younger son demand his inheritance and freedom.
- Watch the son leave, paying particular attention to the father's response. Try to touch his feelings and disappointment.
- With the Spirit's help, connect to the son's immaturity and waste. What would you like to say to him?
- Stand with the father as he watches down the road with hopes of seeing a returning son. What does this tell you about the father.?
- See him run and embrace his son, even while the son is covered in the dirt of his wandering.
- Listen as the father calls for the robe, the ring, and the fatted calf. Watch as the party begins, and touch the father's joy that the one who was thought dead is alive in his arms again.
- Stand to the side and listen as the older son complains about his father's grace.

Notice

- This story is about the Father's acceptance of you as his child. It is a picture of his lavish love and the invitation to celebrate at his table regardless of your behavior.

- What feelings arose as you entered this story with your imagination?
- What does it mean that you are the Father's child, secure, whether you are home in his embrace, wandering in rebellion, or returning to the house of love?
- In what ways has the Father chased after you?
- Notice the way God blesses you with robes, rings, and fatted calves even when you have wandered from his embrace.
- What feelings arise when you think about Christians demanding that you must clean yourself before you eat at God's table?
- In what ways are you still trapped in "washday" theology?
- Notice your emotions when you touch the truth of feasting at the table of the Lord.

Give Thanks

One of the songs of heaven reads,

> Worthy is the Lamb, who was slain,
> to receive power and wealth and wisdom and strength
> and honor and glory and praise! (Rev. 5:12)

Spend time joining your thanks to those praising the Lord in heaven, remembering the grace of Christ that has secured your place at the table of the Lord.

7

ALL THINGS NEW

I'm a sucker when businesses advertise that they are giving away free stuff, like at our local car dealership. Once a year they mail scratch-off cards to area residents, and if you uncover the matching number, you can go into their showroom and receive your grand prize—supposedly.

The flyer includes pictures of big-screen television sets, computers, new cars, and vacation trips to exotic locations. As incentive to visit the showroom, the mailer pictures bundles of cash falling like rain from the sky. Even though I know it is a bait-and-switch ploy, I get hooked every time. I make my way to the dealership and listen to a long pitch about buying a new car before I leave with my special gift. Each time they have handed me a two-dollar bill as I walk out the door!

Scripture says that God pours grace out upon his children for free. The gifts he promises, however, are priceless. They include being chosen as his own, forgiven, adopted, filled with incomparable power, sealed by the Holy Spirit, seated with Christ in heaven with unsearchable riches, and claimed as God's own possession

(Eph. 1–2). All these gifts and much, much more are given—not because you earned his favor, but because Christ came into your heart by faith.

God's lavish grace-gifting is admittedly hard to comprehend, especially in a "you've got to earn it" world. Some of us suspect that grace comes with warnings in small print, statements about keeping rules or else being disqualified. When God says *free* it doesn't actually *mean* free, does it? There has to be a catch somewhere.

Marie Nichol loves the Lord. She serves as a small-group leader in her church and never hides the fact that she is a Christ follower. Marie believes that being born again is the way to enter God's kingdom and does her part to share the gospel. She loves to talk to people about Jesus.

Marie is also obsessive about what she calls "doing enough" for the Lord. She exhausts herself trying to prove that she is worthy of God's love and most days is convinced she is not. She berates herself if she misses her devotions, almost neurotically confesses every mistake she makes, as though her eternal life were at risk if she didn't, and judges herself unmercifully for her perceived weaknesses and imperfections.

Somewhere deep inside, far beneath what she shares with others about Christ, Marie believes her behavior determines her standing with God, for better or for worse. She speaks a great deal about grace, but she isn't confident that the gifts of God are freely given, no payment necessary.

The apostle Paul wrote, "What we have received is not the spirit of the world, but the Spirit who is from God, so that we may understand what God has *freely given* us" (1 Cor. 2:12—emphasis mine). The Lord knew it would be impossible for us to wrap our minds around the claim that God's gifts are "freely given." So God gave us the Holy Spirit to help us understand what "freely given" means for our lives. The phrase is actually quite scandalous when you think about it. Unearned. Undeserved. Lavish. Irrevocable. No strings attached. Just open your heart and receive! Can that kind of grace be real?

God's incomparable gifts belong to you—right now. They are yours regardless of how you behaved yesterday or the mistakes you might make tomorrow. Each grace gifting is part of the extravagant treasure that comes because you are a child of God. These gifts are part of an inheritance of riches you are free to draw from every day. This divine generosity is at the heart of the gospel, the good news that says God is nuts about people everywhere and wants to show it.

Jesus came to this earth to make you whole, not to place performance burdens on your back (John 3:16–17). Think for a moment about how the Bible refers to Jesus. He is the good shepherd who lays down his life for the sheep (John 10:1–18), the vine who gives life to his branches (John 15:1–17), the physician who helps those who are broken (Luke 5:31), the light that shines in the darkness (John 1:5), and the lamb who takes away the sins of the world (John 1:29).

Do you need safe pasture and protection? Do you want the vitality and power of Jesus flowing through your life? Are there places in your life in need of his healing touch? In this world of darkness, would you like some light on the path ahead? Is there sin in your life that is weighing you down? Jesus is the gift of God given to you, the gift that can meet the deepest needs in your life and so much more, the gift that is freely given.

A New Creation

God didn't send Jesus to simply smooth out a few rough spots in your life or provide high-powered spiritual whiteout for all your mistakes. There is far more to God's transforming love than offering you a spiritual makeover. *Jesus came to embed brilliance at the very core of who you are.* There is a brilliance residing in you right now and it is at the heart of all that has been freely given to you through Christ. You have been made new by Jesus. This promised transformation is at the heart of the good news of the kingdom of God. (2 Cor. 5:17; Gal. 6:15).

Granted, my behavior can betray the claim that I am a new creation. After I came to Christ, I looked the same as before, acted pretty much the same as before, and thought a whole lot the way I had before Jesus took me into his heart. When it comes to matters of grace, however, appearances can be deceptive. Deep within my life, Jesus made me a new creation. The exact same way grace has made you a new creation.

Maybe this illustration will help. Imagine there was a time when I was a pig. I had pig appetites, ate pig food, rolled in pig mud, hung out with pig friends, and did everything pigs do. Now imagine that by some miracle, Jesus transformed me into an eagle. In a moment in time, he gave me powerful talons, the heart to soar, eyes to see for miles, wings to catch the wind, and a beauty that defied description.

Now imagine that after I experienced this miraculous transformation, I decided, as an eagle, to go hang out with my old pig pals. Pretty soon, I started eating pig food, rolling in pig mud, acting like a pig, and smelling like a pig. Covered in muck, most people would have assumed that I was a pig.

Standing there displaying my pig-like appearance and behavior, what was I really? I was an eagle—granted, a rather stupid, immature eagle. But my behavior would not have defined my nature, because I had been miraculously changed. I was a new creation because of Jesus.

That is precisely what Paul was telling the Corinthian follow-ers of Jesus. What was true of them is true of you as well. You are now, because of grace, a new creation in Christ Jesus. Changes have taken place that completely redefine who you are and what is true of your now-transformed life.

Your transformation did not happen gradually but occurred miraculously in a moment in time. Learning to live out of what is new about you, however, will take time. With the Spirit's help you can awaken each day to your new life and start to live as the new creation you are. That is why you need the Holy Spirit. He can empower you to live like the "eagle" you have become in Christ.

Remember: Jesus didn't simply remodel the parts of your life that were broken and messed up. He transformed you into a new creation altogether. There is wonder and beauty inside you, part of the incomparable riches of Christ that the Lord has freely bestowed upon your life. Awakening to who you are in Christ will open your heart to a life of incredible freedom and hope.

So What Is New?

Do you remember Marie Nichol? She spent a large part of her life telling people they were special. She didn't, however, believe it about herself. Her obsession with performing for God bordered on pathology, with self-condemning recordings playing over and over in her mind. She knew only these ways to silence the voices of shame: try harder, work longer, and prove to God that she was worthy of love.

Many of us struggle like Marie, in bondage to the all-too-common belief that something is broken deep within, fixed by striving toward a standard of holiness forever an arm's length away. Marie needed a spiritual awakening, an eye-opening spiritual experience that would enable her to see what it means to be a new creation in Jesus Christ.

So the question you may have is "What exactly is new about me?" To begin with, you have a *new nature* (you share the likeness of Jesus). *Nature* is defined as the essential characteristics and quality of a species. As unbelievable as it may sound, you now share the essential characteristics and qualities of Jesus at the core of your being. Think about that for a few minutes. If someone asked, "What kind of a person are you?," you could answer, "A Jesus kind of person, part of his species." God has given you everything you need to successfully live the Christian life, and besides amazing promises from God, you actually now share the nature of Jesus himself (2 Pet. 1:3–4)

When you were taken into the heart of Christ, a change took place at the core of your being. It was a transformation as dramatic as being changed from a pig to an eagle. As Peter wrote, God has given you everything you need to live a good and godly life, as well as providing you with amazing promises about his care. You were also given a completely new nature, with characteristics and qualities of Jesus placed inside you.

Where once your nature was broken, which bent you toward sin, you now share the nature of Christ Jesus himself. Even on your worst day, if someone were able to peel back your body and look deep inside, they would be stunned by your brilliance. They would see the light of Jesus shining forth from you. His glory and his goodness are now reflected in your glory and your goodness, freely given to you by the lavish grace of God himself.

Every time you're tempted toward self-rejection and contempt, when the voices in your head tell you that you're not enough, when you believe if people really knew you they would reject you, stop and ask the Holy Spirit to remind you of what Christ has made eternally true of you. You are a special kind of being, touched by the divine, a reflection of the very nature of Jesus Christ.

You also have a *new identity*—you are a cherished child of God. People everywhere are always asking in one way or another, "Who am I?" They are beaten down as they struggle to secure their uniqueness through possessions, performance, appearance, achievement, titles, and professions. You, however, are able to rest secure in the fact that you are a child of God. One of the main reasons Jesus came to earth was so you would be forever identified as his child (Gal. 4:4–7). Your identity as God's child is the basis of every unique and wonderful thing about you.

The deepest longings of your life can be met because you are God's child. No more exhausting yourself performing, pleasing, achieving, or acquiring. You don't have to fight to be loved, accepted, secure, or significant. Your value is no longer attached to your appearance, job, relationships, or possessions.

You have a permanent seat at the table of the Lord. Your deepest desires can be filled at his feast, where goodness and mercy flow in abundance. You are a favored child. Jesus alone defines you; no one else. When the dark harmony of voices tries to tell you what you are not, let the Holy Spirit awaken you to who you are. If the devil speaks, shout back, "I am a child of God and that settles it for me."

Three Great Changes

Centuries ago, God spoke to the prophet Ezekiel and told him that in the distant future there would be specific blessings he would give to the people of God. At the time, God's people were repeatedly wandering away from his love and care. The Lord said there would come a day when he would work three great changes so that people would stay close to him (Ezek. 36:25–27).

First, God promised to give people a *new heart* (responsive to the love of God). He wasn't talking about a physical organ, but the center of human affection and compassion. God told Ezekiel that sin had hardened people's hearts. As a result, they didn't show kindness and love to one another or maintain their affection for God. Their hardened hearts made them a selfish and rebellious people.

God promised a new day, however, when he would transform people's lives. He would, by grace, give people a new heart so that they could live according to the virtues and values of the kingdom. Jesus was alluding to this when he talked to Nicodemus about being born again (John 3). He was pointing to a supernaturally empowered newness of heart.

All the values and virtues of the kingdom are placed like seeds within you right now. You don't have to pray, "Lord, make me loving, kind, patient, caring." Those possibilities are already present, abiding in you the same way apple trees abide in that small apple seed you can hold in your hand. Granted, the fruits of the Spirit need to be nurtured to life, which is precisely what the Holy Spirit longs to do. A more precise prayer would be, "Lord, let the love, kindness, patience, and care you have planted within me grow to your glory."

All this and more are the result of the deep change God has worked in your life. You just need to ask the Holy Spirit to destroy all the defenses you have put up because of past hurt and awaken the love of the kingdom that abides in your new heart because of Jesus.

You not only have a new nature (you share the likeness of Christ), a new identity (you are a cherished child of God), and new heart (you are responsive to the love of God)—you also have a *new spirit* (Ezek. 36:25–27). *You have a new spiritual openness.*

When Jesus spoke with Nicodemus, he told him that seeing and participating in the kingdom of God required a new birth (John 3:1–8)—not a physical birth, but rather a spiritual birth.

When each of us humans was created, God breathed his life into our spirit. It was the place of communion and intimacy with the Father. Unfortunately, because of sin and brokenness, that spiritual center died, which contributed to wandering away from God. People became incapable of following the Lord's commands, which in turn kept them from resting in the fullness of God's love and blessings.

God promised a day would come when he would give people a new spirit, a place where they could again fellowship with him. This new spirit is part of the spiritual awakening Jesus made possible when you entrusted your life to him. It is part of the wonder of the new you.

There is one more aspect of the new creation promise that may be the most thrilling of gift of all. Knowing that God's people had trouble following him, he decided to place his Holy Spirit inside of his children as a *new helper*. God knows that we cannot walk through this broken world in our strength, so long ago he promised that there would be a day when the Holy Spirit would live inside his children.

John the Baptist once said, "After me comes the one more powerful than I, the straps of whose sandals I am not worthy to stoop down and untie. I baptize you with water, but he will baptize you with the Holy Spirit" (Mark 1:7–8). John was speaking of Jesus. Later, the Lord promised his followers that they would have the indwelling presence of the Holy Spirit as their constant strength and help (John 14:17).

The Spirit's indwelling presence is part of God's great gift of grace, freely given. The Holy Spirit brings dimensions of authority and power to your life that were previously reserved for the chosen few. Please consider this breathtaking truth: the Holy Spirit, who raised Christ from the dead, is very much alive inside you (Eph. 1:18–20)! Regardless of what the dark voices may say, you are a force to be reckoned with.

I remember one day listening as Marie Nichol told me about everything that was wrong with her and why she needed to work hard at being a better person. As I listened, a phrase kept playing in my mind, a silly phrase from my childhood, teasingly recited about some secret knowledge. "I know something you don't know." It inspired me to look beyond Marie's words to a deeper truth about her life. She was filled with wonder and brilliance, a new creation in Christ Jesus. What she needed was a fresh awakening of the Holy Spirit in order to see what others suspected all along. She didn't know she was an amazing person, but I did because God said it was true. She possessed the brilliance of Christ.

You too are no ordinary person. You are a new creation in Christ Jesus. You are his beloved. There are dimensions to your wonder that defy description. God's gifts to you, freely given, are like presents spread lavishly beneath a Christmas tree. You are graced with "newness" and never again need exhaust yourself trying to measure up to be loved and accepted. You are nothing less than a treasure of grace. What you need, as with Marie and me, is an awakening of the Holy Spirit. That happens when you position yourself in the presence of God's Spirit. There he can help you see the lavish grace God has so generously deposited in your life.

EXPERIENTIAL

Many things vie for your time. The truth is, not everything you do contributes to the release of wonder God has placed deep within your life. We will look at some of these misplaced investments more specifically in upcoming chapters. Chose now to regularly enter a sacred time with the Lord. It is one of those rare investments that you cannot afford to neglect. It positions you for awakening, the raising of spiritual awareness, and the empowerment of the Holy Spirit, who enables you to live out who you are in Christ. I encourage you to go to your quiet place, take a posture of receptivity, and breathe in the Spirit's presence.

Remain in the Light

I invite you to ponder three scriptures. The first is an Old Testament text that was a prophetic promise about newness in your life.

> I will sprinkle clean water on you, and you will be clean;
> I will cleanse you from all your impurities and from all
> your idols. I will give you a new heart and put a new
> spirit in you; I will remove from you your heart of stone
> and give you a heart of flesh. And I will put my Spirit in
> you and move you to follow my decrees and be careful
> to keep my laws. (Ezek. 36:25–27)

The second scripture is from the writings of the apostle Paul:

> When someone becomes a Christian, he becomes a
> brand new person inside. He is not the same anymore. A
> new life has begun!
> All these new things are from God who brought us
> back to himself through what Christ Jesus did. And God

has given us the privilege of urging everyone to come into his favor and be reconciled to him. For God was in Christ, restoring the world to himself, no longer counting men's sins against them but blotting them out. This is the wonderful message he has given us to tell others. (2 Cor. 5:17–19 TLB)

Finally, I want you to turn to the first two chapters of Ephesians. With pen in hand, spend time writing down everything this scripture says is true of you because of Christ. Note the phrase *freely given* found in chapter one. You have, as verse three says, everything you need to live the life God intended because of the grace Jesus has deposited in your life. Spend time contemplating each truth, confessing what these phrases are describing about you.

Imagine Prophetically

Please remember that imagination is a gift from the Lord. It enables you to experience the truth of Scripture, encoding God's Word deeply into your mind. Ask the Holy Spirit to help you see, feel, and sense the power of what God's Word is saying in the passages shared in this chapter.

As you read through the first two chapters of Ephesians, you discovered several words and phrases that are true of you as a new creation in Christ. Prayerfully look over the list below.

- Chosen
- Forgiven
- Lavished upon
- Sealed by the Spirit
- God's possession

- Adopted
- Given incomparable power
- Seated with Christ
- The dwelling of God

Please ask the Holy Spirit to cause one of these truths to stand out above the rest, as though suddenly written in red letters. Once you sense that word or phrase, invite the Spirit to use your imagination to show what God is saying to you, as though you were watching a motion picture of it happening.

Notice

- What did you experience as the Holy Spirit used your imagination in the exercise above?
- Pay attention to what you felt, sensed, saw, and learned.
- Notice your body's response as you engaged with the Lord.
- What feelings arise when you consider the magnitude of "newness" placed within your life? Take time to think about each truth.
- New nature (bearer of the likeness of Christ)
- New identity (cherished child of God)
- New heart (responsive to the love of God)
- New spirit (open place of spiritual awareness)
- New helper (the abiding presence of the Holy Spirit)
- What impact does the truth of your "newness" have upon your sense of self-worth?
- What has the Holy Spirit revealed regarding God's love for you?

Give Thanks

The psalmist wrote,

> Give thanks to the LORD, for he is good;
>> his love endures forever. (Ps. 118:1)

What is your own psalm of thanks for all the Lord has done in your life? Spend time writing it out in your journal, and share it with a friend. Try turning it into your own "new song" and prayerfully sing your thanks to God for all he has "freely given" you because of Christ Jesus.

WHAT BLINDS YOU TO WHO YOU REALLY ARE?

8

THE REALITY OF SPIRITUAL WARFARE

I t was a typical Friday evening. We shoveled down our dinner and, like thoroughbreds pawing the ground at the Belmont Stakes, leapt from our cracked, vinyl-covered kitchen chairs and rushed to our assigned posts. Mom turned on the black-and-white television program and planted herself on the corner of the threadbare couch.

My sister, Bonny, stood at the screen door, her hair teased until it looked downright angry, as Dad, clad in a stained sleeveless tee shirt, set the worn wooden ladder on the side of the house and climbed onto the roof, making his way to the antennae strapped onto the stone chimney.

I stood in the yard where I could see both Dad and Bonny, part of the human conduit passing messages from Mom on the couch to Dad clinging to the roof. Our television set picked up two stations, only if the stars were properly aligned.

And so it began. Mom turned to channel eleven, and Bonny shouted. "Mom says it's all fuzzy."

"It's fuzzy Dad, all fuzzy" I repeated, my head bent backward to watch him grip the chimney in one hand and antennae in the other. Dad didn't respond, so I said it more loudly: "Mom said it's fuzzy!"

"I heard you the first time!" he shouted. "It's *always* fuzzy! Why do you think I'm up here in the first place?" Grumbling and head-shaking followed as Dad repositioned the aluminum spines.

Back and forth it went, "A little more . . . too far . . . stop right there . . . back up . . . you had it . . . ." There was plenty of cussing, eye-rolling, and shouting until Mom finally announced that the picture was good.

There was something almost religious about this routine on Friday nights, my family huddled shoulder to shoulder on secondhand furniture like saints squeezed into a wooden pew at church. It wasn't the second coming we were anticipating but rather the beginning of "Studio Wrestling," a no-holds-barred battle royal between large sweaty men clad in skin-tight costumes that matched their terrifying names.

There were evil giants like Gorilla Monsoon, Killer Kowalski, and George the Animal Steele trying to unseat the reigning champion, Bruno Sanmartino. It was good against evil, right battling wrong, the gavel of justice hammered down with splattered blood and cauliflower ears.

Week by week the evil guys dominated matches with illegal holds, eye-gouging, misdirection, and deception. But just as the referee began to lift his arm to declare a bad guy the winner, a good guy would get a surge of energy, slip out from under the gargantuan monster, pin evil to the mat, and win the day—bleeding, mistreated, every ounce of energy spent, the arising conqueror proving yet again that playing fair defeats even the wiliest foe!

Serious Business

I wish life were like "Studio Wrestling," but it's not. You're engaged in a great battle, neither choreographed nor staged. You don't have the luxury of sitting in an easy chair and watching. Every day, you're at center ring, wrestling "against the rulers, against the authorities, against the powers of this dark world and against spiritual forces of evil in the heavenly realms" (Eph. 6:12). Sometimes it's impossible to tell the good guys from the bad, and you had better have your eyes wide open to the tactics that evil uses to destroy you.

A power is aligned against you, and I assure you that it's not God. Satan has rallied his minions to mar every good thing God has made on this earth. You are the crown of God's creation, so the crosshairs are centered squarely on you.

British scholar and Anglican priest David Watson told us in class that where God is at work, Satan is equally active. The evil one despises image-bearers, so that means you. In subtle and overt ways, he tries to convince you that you don't measure up, all the while strategizing to destroy the wonder God has deposited into your life. Satan's favorite tools are doubt, discouragement, and deception. Nowhere are his attacks more laser-focused than upon the brilliance that resides inside you. The evil one sees your gifting but works desperately to keep you from ever catching a glimpse.

It takes a spiritual awakening to discern the movement of the enemy. The agents of evil are invisible, never play fair, grant no quarter, and traffic in deception and lies. Good guys don't always wear white, and evil does not show up clad in hooded black robes carrying a scythe. Darkness is often masked as light and pounces when you're least suspecting, hitting hard where you're most susceptible.

This is why I've been so angry about my beautiful young friend dying at her own hand. Satan goes that far. You must learn to stand against the evil one's efforts to harm the children God cherishes.

Know Your Enemy

Have you heard the adage "I'm my own worst enemy"? Don't believe it. Your worst enemy is the evil one, and it's time you understand that. Something is seriously wrong in this world, which is why the apostle Paul wrote about the nature of the evil one and the battle we face.

First, he said your struggle is not against flesh and blood (Eph. 6:12). Let's not pass by this insight too quickly, or we will end up attacking people—when it's actually the destructive power *behind* the misguided that we need to combat.

This is not an easy task. A few years ago, a person made it his business to attack me and worked to destroy the ministry of healing I was part of. His efforts were relentless—and by all appearances effective. I made the mistake of seeing him as my enemy and concentrated my efforts on combating him.

The Lord reminded me of what Greg Boyd said at a seminar I sponsored: "If it has flesh and blood, it is not my enemy." That truth should keep us from vilifying people, who are in themselves broken. This does not eliminate human responsibility, but it should keep us aware that we image-bearers need to learn to get along.

The apostle Paul also wrote that evil is unseen, in the form of spiritual rulers, authorities, dark powers, and spiritual forces (Eph. 6:12). Imagine for a moment that you had a powerful human enemy who wanted to harm you. Now imagine this person could make himself or herself invisible, sneak up on you, take a swipe at you, even lay in wait for you, and you would have no idea he or she was around. That would be frightening and impossible to combat. Paul wants us to be aware that there are powerful invisible players on the field just like that, and we need the Lord's help to discern their presence and defend ourselves.

The Devil's Tactics

Grandma Della Saunders was a woman who had a profound impact upon my spiritual life. She was a saint who raised her grandson Brian, one of my boyhood friends. Grandma began to influence my spiritual development when I was still a rebellious teenager. She called me her grandson, and on almost every occasion we were together, she ended by saying, "Remember, son, Grandma is on the battlefield for her Lord."

She realized something every believer needs to know: every morning, you place your feet on a battlefield in a war with unseen spiritual forces. Four tactics of the enemy stand out—places where he loves to attack us. These are his favorite hunting grounds:

1. He attacks your identity.
2. He goes after unhealed emotional wounds.
3. He appeals to unmet longings and disordered desires.
4. He tries to convince you that God is neither loving nor good.

The first attack is ground zero—your identity as a child of God.

Satan works tirelessly to convince you that you're not enough, defining you as broken and irreparable. He spews constant threats that if people really knew you, they would reject you. He attacks your thoughts, uses the words of others against you, and characterizes God as angry and displeased. He wants you to either rebel against God or wear yourself out trying to earn his favor. He does not want you to awaken to how secure and cherished you are as God's child.

Jesus was weak and vulnerable after spending forty days fasting and praying alone in a wasteland, a bake-oven wilderness where snakes and scorpions fought to survive (Luke 4:1–13). Satan had been watching Jesus, waiting for the moment when weakness gave room to dismantle everything the Father had declared to be true. When the time was right, Satan struck, and he aimed precisely at the Lord's identity.

Two times the devil began his assault with the phrase "If you are the Son of God." What he tried with Jesus he most certainly will do with you. If he can get you to question your security as a child of God, he can lure you into all kinds of destructive behaviors. Awareness of being a child of God is the foundation of self-acceptance and strength. Remember: no one gets to define you but Jesus—not even you!

That is not Satan's only strategy. He capitalizes upon every vulnerability you have, not the least of which are unresolved emotional wounds of the past. I once heard author LeAnne Payne say that Satan makes a nest in our wounds. How true that is! This is the second tactic the enemy will use against you. What remains unhealed within you becomes the terrain Satan attacks to bring despair and heartache to your life. It doesn't matter if what remains unhealed is the equivalent of an emotional paper cut or a slash that is soul deep. If he can harass you there, he will.

Cathy Tustin's life was driven by a single statement made by her mother: "Dad and I don't believe you need any education beyond high school. Whatever money we have, it will go to your brothers for college." That became Cathy's defining statement. She wasn't worth it. Regardless of what she achieved, which included two academic degrees, or what she accomplished, being named head of a financial firm, those words defined her. Cathy was hurt, she was angry, she was bitter, and she believed they were right. Satan used that wound to launch attack after attack against Cathy.

He uses the same tactic on you. If there is a past trauma, emotional wound, false belief, or ungrieved loss in your life, Satan will try using it to destroy you. He will throw it up in your face, agitate you, and try to get you preoccupied with the pain. Satan wants you bitter, angry, exhausted, and hanging on by an emotional thread. If he can keep you focused on the pain, you will never discover the strength of Christ in the place where wounds now dominate your thoughts.

God created you with a longing for love, safety, belonging, security, purpose, and understanding, and he wants to be the source of satisfying those desires. Unfortunately, in a broken world, unmet longings become the feeding ground for the evil one. If he senses emptiness, he will try to lure you into behaviors that promise satisfaction but in the end break you. What Satan dangles in front of you might shine, but its purpose is to hook and control you. Ask any addict or person trapped in a harmful dependency, and he or she will tell you it's true. Desire turned away from God brings bondage. Satan knows that, and that is his third tactic.

I grew up at a time when there was tremendous fear of nuclear holocaust, one of the tens of thousands of children who spent time beneath desks practicing for doomsday. It seemed there was the constant threat of sudden and unmerciful annihilation, birthing thoughts on restless nights that I dare not close my eyes since death was a blink in time away. The idea of entering eternity brought no comfort to me, because the belief in our home was that God had his own hammer and sickle, wielded without restraint upon anyone who dared cross him. The next life seemed to offer only more of the same.

The evil one trades in such deception. He has been working to get people to question the goodness and love of God ever since that very first "Did God really say . . . ?" (Gen. 3:1). When possible, he enlists the Lord's own people to characterize God as capricious and withholding, far more generous with wrath than mercy. Worst of all, he tries to take advantage of every loss and disappointment, whispering into the minds of the grieving that God is ruthless, cruel, and uncaring. The evil one knows that questioning the character of God makes a person easy prey, so he's relentless.

Identity insecurity, emotional wounds, unmet core longings, and distortions about God are prime targets for the evil one. Knowing that is a great first start. What you need now are action steps that will help you resist the devil and draw near to God in this great battle.

So What Can You Do?

You are more than a conqueror because of the love of Christ (Rom. 8:37.) God is on your side, and he is far greater than the one who is against you (1 John 4:4). These two truths provide a rock-solid foundation for you to stand upon against the evil one. Personalize each statement, and start each day declaring, "I am more than a conqueror because of Christ. His presence with me is far stronger than any attack the evil one can bring my way."

I also suggest building a practical strategy of spiritual warfare from the teachings of the apostle Paul in 1 Corinthians 16:13–14.

Be on Your Guard

Paul knew the enemy is always on the prowl. So he issued a warning for Christians to be diligent and watchful. One of the most dangerous lapses in wartime is for a soldier to fall asleep on watch. It could cost him and others their lives. So it is in spiritual warfare.

Centuries ago, the great Chinese general Sun Tzu wrote, "If you know your enemy and know yourself, you need not fear the result of a hundred battles. If you know yourself and not the enemy, for every victory gained you will also suffer defeat. If you know neither yourself nor the enemy, you will succumb in every battle."

Being on guard means knowing your enemy—and knowing your-self well enough to strengthen places of personal vulnerability.

Being on guard means giving attention to your choices, staying away from activities that give ground to the enemy, surrounding yourself with God's people, and reading God's Word. It means being extra cautious where you have stumbled in the past and being honest about areas of weakness and getting help. It means protecting your heart, keeping Jesus at the center, and guarding your mind, filling it with whatever is true, right, noble, pure, lovely, admirable, excellent, and praiseworthy (Phil. 4:8). This is war, and these are the weapons that can save your life.

Stand Firm in the Faith

You must be confident in what Christ Jesus has done for you. The security of your identity as a child of God, and the truth of Christ's extravagant grace poured out upon you, must be hardwired into your mind. "Firm in the faith" means that you are a Jesus person through and through. You know what has been freely given and are confident that you can face all things because of Jesus (Phil. 4:13). Faith does not always come easily, and it will certainly be challenged by the evil one. But hold firm.

Here are several truths that may help you:

- Jesus defeated and disarmed the demons of darkness at the cross (Col. 2:15).
- You have been rescued from the domain of darkness (Col. 1:13).
- By the cross, Christ has canceled every debt you owed. You are free! (Col. 2:14).
- You are seated with Christ in heaven as a sign of your authority (Eph. 2:6).

- Jesus has made you a child of God and filled you with the Spirit (Gal. 4:4–6).
- God intends to crush Satan under your feet (Rom. 16:20).

You can pull out these promises like a sword whenever the evil one comes near.

Be Strong and Be Courageous

I can be a bit of a wimp. That's why I'm grateful that God is not asking me to use my strength and courage to combat the evil one. Being strong and courageous is about being empowered by the Holy Spirit, allowing him to help you resist the evil one.

Jesus relied upon the Holy Spirit and so should you. When Paul called Christians to be strong in the Lord and the strength of his might (Eph. 6:10), he was encouraging you to be confident in everything Jesus has done for you and to rely upon the strength of the Holy Spirit.

The same power that raised Christ from the dead abides in you, so turn to the Spirit quickly and often. Use this powerful prayer when things get tough: "Help!"

When your mind is racing with negative thoughts and fears, follow Paul's advice and ask the Spirit to take over your thinking (Rom. 8:6). You are not on your own in this battle.

Don't go looking for a fight with the devil. But when he comes, remember that you have Jesus on your side. Stand your ground. Confront the enemy, declare the truth that you are a child of God, that you're seated with Christ, and that he has no business messing with you. When the evil one threatens, draw close to the Lord and resist! (James 4:7–10). When Satan comes your way, stand next to Jesus and tell the devil to go in Jesus's name. Do this every day, countless times a day, and as you do, your confidence in Christ will grow, and the threats of the evil one will diminish.

Do Everything in Love

Notice what Jesus was doing when you read about him in the Gospels. Most of the time, he was demonstrating love, teaching about love, or commanding his followers to show some love. He calls us to love one another, love our neighbor, love the poor, love the hungry, love the naked, love the stranger, and even love our enemies. This is not shallow sentimentality he is suggesting, a meaningless wink or nod. Jesus expects us to live by the law of love, even when it means personal sacrifice. Love is both the way of the kingdom and the way of the cross.

Love is not something soft or sentimental but a powerful force against the evil one. When most Christians think about spiritual warfare, images of long prayer meetings, deliverance sessions, and direct confrontations with demons come to mind. That can be the strategy in some cases. However, there is something you can do every day that holds nuclear power against evil: choose to live by the virtues and values of the kingdom of love. Teilhard de Chardin wrote, "The day will come when, after harnessing the space, the winds, the tides, gravitation, we shall harness for God the energies of love. And, in that day, for the second time in history of the world, [we] will have discovered fire."

Forgiving someone who has offended you is an act of spiritual warfare. If you show kindness, choose to be generous, extend mercy to a person who has been mean to you, call a friend who is lonely, or invite a hurting person for coffee, you are engaging in boots-on-the-ground spiritual warfare. A moment of tenderness, compassion, humility, selflessness, and patience holds revolutionary power. Gratitude is a powerful weapon. It lifts our eyes to God and thwarts the devil's efforts to get us locked on to our circumstances. Every act of kingdom love brings light into this dark world. Where there is light, the evil one is powerless. Bring more light!

You are a force to be reckoned with. God knows it and welcomes you to a new kingdom awakening, the unleashing of the wonder of you. Satan knows it too and will do anything to keep you in bondage. Say yes to the Lord and stand against darkness in the power of Christ your Lord.

EXPERIENTIAL

Regardless of how busy he became, Jesus always slipped away to quiet places to be with the Father. It gave him strength, refocused his attention, reprioritized his time, and restored his soul. Your choice to do the same is a mark of maturity, not weakness. Value sacred time and sacred space. Engaging in this spiritual exercise opens you to the experience of his presence—so essential to your life, especially in times of spiritual warfare.

Remain in the Light

Slowly and prayerfully read this familiar passage on spiritual warfare. Invite the Holy Spirit to be your helper, revealing truths you may never have noticed before.

A final word: Be strong in the Lord and in his mighty power. Put on all of God's armor so that you will be able to stand firm against all strategies of the devil. For we are not fighting against flesh-and-blood enemies, but against evil rulers and authorities of the unseen world, against mighty powers in this dark world, and against evil spirits in the heavenly places.

Therefore, put on every piece of God's armor so you will be able to resist the enemy in the time of evil. Then after the battle you will still be standing firm. Stand your ground, putting on the belt of truth and the body armor of God's righteousness. For shoes, put on the peace that comes from the Good News so that you will be fully prepared. In addition to all of these, hold up the shield of faith to stop the fiery arrows of the devil. Put on salvation as your helmet, and take the sword of the Spirit, which is the word of God.

Pray in the Spirit at all times and on every occasion. Stay alert and be persistent in your prayers for all believers everywhere.

And pray for me, too. Ask God to give me the right words so I can boldly explain God's mysterious plan that the Good News is for Jews and Gentiles alike. I am in chains now, still preaching this message as God's ambassador. So pray that I will keep on speaking boldly for him, as I should. (Eph. 6:10–20 NLT)

Imagine Prophetically

Allow the Holy Spirit to engage your imagination. It will help you embrace and respond to what Paul is teaching in this text. Be open to seeing this scripture in new and relevant ways.

Invite the Spirit to show you what "strong in the Lord and in his mighty power" would look like for you.

Imagine the great battle in which you engage against the spiritual forces, which Paul writes of in this text.

Slowly put on each piece of the armor of God:

- Belt of truth
- Breastplate of righteousness
- Shoes of peace
- Shield of faith
- Helmet of salvation
- Sword of the Spirit

Ask the Spirit to show you what keeping alert, persevering, and praying looks like for you.

Notice

- What feelings have arisen as you engage this scripture with your imagination?
- Do you notice any body tension, and if so, what is happening?
- Why is it important that you be strong in the Lord? What does that mean to you?
- In what ways did you experience the strength of "his mighty power" as you imagined this text? What difference does that make in spiritual warfare?
- What emotions do you experience when you consider that your unseen enemy is spiritual as well as powerful?
- What did you experience as you put on each piece of the armor of God?
- How might doing that daily help you?
- What did the Holy Spirit teach you about being alert?
- What roles will perseverance and prayer now take in your life?

Give Thanks

The psalmist repeatedly called God's people to praise and more than once linked praise to spiritual warfare, as in the following scripture:

> May the praise of God be in their mouths
> and a double-edged sword in their hands. (Ps. 149:6)

Every word of thanksgiving is an act of warfare, pressing back darkness and inviting in kingdom light. I encourage you to journal your praise as well as share it with other people, part of "boots on the ground" warfare against the evil one. Spend some time singing a song of praise as a way of being grateful to the Lord.

9

THE MESSAGE THAT
YOU ARE NOT ENOUGH

It is best when certain things are burned or thrown away—especially report cards from high school. I had thought mine were relegated to the trash bin of history, when they suddenly emerged during a time when my adult children went rummaging through my mother's things after she passed away. After years of keeping that part of my past in the dark, I had a boatload of explaining to do.

I wasn't much of a student in high school. It wasn't a matter of aptitude, but attitude. My constant restlessness, simmering anger, and emotional wounding, connected in part to a parent's comment about my mental abilities, caused me to check out. I did the bare minimum, which for the most part meant below-average grades, sometimes way below—well, *most* of the time way below.

At the end of my junior year, the principal called me into his office. I was on the student council, normally reserved for brainiacs, and he was interested in my plans for the future. I mentioned college. "Son," he sighed, "I encourage you to consider a trade school. At the rate you are going, you may not get out of high school, let alone into college."

I applied to a bunch of colleges and received the same response, which I interpreted as "You've got to be kidding. Is this a joke?" Undeterred, especially with the military looming, I kept sending in applications until one day I received a letter in the mail that said, "Congratulations. You have been accepted . . ."

Despite horrible grades, a low SAT score, no athletic value, a principal who believed I wouldn't get in, and hope virtually gone, I was accepted. "Congratulations" translated into a declaration of my worth as a human being. "I am acceptable."

At least for one shining moment, I was enough. I could chime in when friends talked about where they were enrolled, share big plans about living away from home, and pretend that I knew about majors and degrees. I could tell the world that I was going to college, no longer relegated to the back row in life. I had an official letter from an accredited college that proved it. I was accepted.

Most of us are raised in cultures that connect identity security with being enough—or not. With some people, being enough is the foundation of individual uniqueness and acceptability. It defines what is special about you and what gets you a seat at the table. People who are enough have what it takes. They get to play. The losers, who are *not* enough, must limp away, forced to be content in the shadows of life.

You had to measure up to get a seat at the men's table in my family. The calculus included hunting and fishing abilities, fast cars, sexual exploits, and stories that proved you were tough. In my high school, you had to be smart enough to be in the honor society, athletic enough to be in the letterman club, popular enough to be in student government, attractive enough to hang with the cool kids, and in some cases bad enough to run with the hoods. My experience in high school was a microcosm of the world.

Life seems forever divided into A people and B people, number Ones and number Twos. The As get to play, and the Ones get the recognition. Everyone else must work harder, hoping that someday, in some place, they will be allowed to sit at the table and enjoy the good life, at least for a while—as long as they are enough.

Being enough is connected to personal value, self-worth, receiving respect, and most definitely acceptability. Only those who are enough, by whatever standard a group defines, belong. Since belonging is important, people strive to measure up, which in the end beats them down all the more. Believing "I am not enough" will break a person's spirit, let alone his or her heart.

It can also cause people to walk on eggshells for fear of being exposed. When acceptance is based on a person's performance, and that performance is questioned, they respond by either exploding or imploding. Take my friend Bobby. He's a good guy, loves people, and goes out of his way to help others. The other day he called to talk about a blowup he had with his son. It was bad. His son accidentally stepped on an emotional landmine in his dad's life, commenting on an inconsistency he perceived in his dad's behavior. Bobby perceived that his son was saying he didn't measure up, and he lost it. This has been a pattern for Bobby. Whenever he senses criticism, he swells up and goes ballistic to regain ground. He's an exploder.

I understand Bobby's reactivity as that was my style as well. There are others who, instead of *exploding*, *imploding* whenever someone bumps up against their insecurity. They shrink back instead of swelling up and run to a place of hiding. Their withdrawal is as much a defense mechanism as Bobby's explosion, but it is characterized by cowering, essentially agreeing instead of pushing back. Self-rejection and self-punishment follow, and people who implode often end up being harder on themselves than others ever intended to be.

Believing you are not enough is a heavy burden to bear. It leads to destructive behaviors and disconnected relationships. Far too many people, particularly God's people, are weighed down with expectations that they could never attain in the first place. We certainly want to encourage people to turn to Christ to find security, but is the church always a safe place to go when the burden of being enough chafes against the soul?

Where Does the Church Stand?

Where does the church stand on the question of you being enough? Do you need to measure up to gain God's approval? Do you need to be enough in order to be accepted by God? Is "enough" the standard for entrance into his kingdom? If so, what are the exact requirements you must meet to be enough? Are there prerequisites before blessings flow? Do you have to measure up in order to be secure with God?

Too many churches build their model of Christian maturity upon the expectation that you must measure up, be enough, or else. They believe discipleship begins with understanding who you need to *be* as a real Christian. Being enough is the starting place for their acceptance.

I like to think of churches that hold this position as "box" churches. People on the inside of the box are God's special people. They belong. Inside-the-box people get blessings, are forgiven, and receive promises of a good and preferred future. They are given special gifts by God because they measure up. They understand what is required of them and strive to achieve. Members of "box" churches are taught that people on the outside of the box are headed for a really bad time. God is angry with outsiders and looks forward to the day when he doesn't have to put up with them anymore.

Leaders of box churches make it clear that to get on the inside, and stay on the inside, people must attain their narrowly defined standards. People need to believe exactly what they believe, behave the way they behave, and do the things they deem important. Those who prove they measure up are welcomed, while those who do not must stay out. Membership in box churches is restricted to men and women who are worthy of the church's embrace.

Most box churches keep a list of what "real Christians" believe and what "real Christians do." They then hold that list up like a magnifying glass to examine who is acceptable and who is not. There is no shortage of judgment and shame in a box church, doled out to keep people striving to be better and do better.

Box churches traffic in statements about how A people and number Ones receive the promises of God. They are the folks who get God's goodies. While box churches use language that appears to be Christian, the effect on people is not the peace and rest Christ promised. Members end up feeling exhausted from the performance demands, anxious, wondering if they are doing enough to be secure with God. They grow bitter, because no matter what they have done, there is always more required. The threat of judgment hangs over people like a coming storm, causing people to hide their struggles, forcing them to face brokenness alone.

Know Who You Are

Christian discipleship actually begins not by understanding who you need to be but by knowing who you *are* in Christ. The devil, the world, and even some churches may sing a different tune, but don't make the mistake of harmonizing with their dark melody.

You are a child of God, a new creation, and the masterpiece of the Father's creative love. You are a walking icon of God, touched by the transforming work of Jesus. These truths provide a rock-solid foundation upon which you can stand. You are God's cherished child. Christ redeemed your life and you are free, now and forever.

One day, John the Baptist was calling people to repentance, baptizing them in the Jordan river. He told the crowd that God's kingdom was near and now was the time to come home to God's house of love. John was preparing the way for the coming of Jesus, and soon, Jesus would announce that the kingdom, God's reign and rule, had arrived on earth (Mark 1:9–28). God's kingdom, unlike the oppressive rule of Satan, would be a place of generosity, grace, mercy, and acceptance. The broken and bruised would be welcomed and wanderers embraced as they returned home to their Father.

As John was preaching and baptizing, religious leaders gathered on the banks of the Jordan to watch and ridicule. They were "box" people, standing above the crowd, looking down their noses at people they believed to be the dirty, unwashed of life. These religious hardliners bragged about being top-tiered people with God—"A" people and number Ones. They were the self-appointed scorekeepers who bragged about rule-keeping, proof that they had earned their way with God. They were sure that the losers knee-deep in Jordan River mud were classic outsiders.

John the Baptist saw Jesus coming, declared him to be the Lamb of God, and promised that someday soon Jesus would be baptizing people with the Holy Spirit (John 1:26–36). Though reluctant, John baptized Jesus in the Jordan, right under the turned-up noses of the religious know-it-alls up on the bank. Something amazing followed. As Jesus rose from beneath the river, water dancing before his eyes like sunlit diamonds, the heavens opened, and God spoke. He called Jesus his chosen and beloved Son, and then the Holy Spirit, in the form of a dove, settled upon him (Matt. 3:13–17).

Loved, Chosen, Empowered

Loved. Chosen. Empowered. What Christian doesn't want to hear those words? They are the ultimate declaration of acceptance, of respect, of value, of being enough. Sadly, many of us wonder what we need to do so that we will hear God say we are loved, chosen, and empowered. We slip right back into the trap of "box" church thinking.

Look closely at the story of the baptism of Jesus. What had Jesus accomplished prior to this event? According to the Gospels, nothing. There were no miracles, no signs or wonders, no ministry to the broken and bruised, nothing that would identify him as a spiritual leader. As far as anyone there knew, Jesus was a small-town carpenter caring for his mother and siblings. Any suggestion otherwise was based on fable, not fact.

Notice also that Jesus did not choose to be numbered among the religious superstars when he arrived at the Jordan River. He didn't stand on the bank with the elite or isolate himself from the broken masses who were wading waist-deep into the water. Jesus chose to be numbered among the sinners. He was shoulder to shoulder with the beat-up and bruised that day, returning to the embrace of God through the humble act of repentance.

Before Jesus had done anything to prove his worth, and while numbered among the sinners, God declared him loved, chosen, and empowered. God's words were not the result of something he did or achieved. They were not a reward for measuring up to some predetermined standard. God was declaring his love for Jesus as his Son, and in so doing he revealed his love for you as well.

More than heaven opened on the day Jesus was baptized. The Father's heart broke wide open to all his children, spilling out unconditional love. Jesus stood in for us in the waters of baptism and received the eternal declaration of God's affection and acceptance for all his children.

You are loved. You are chosen. You are empowered by the Holy Spirit. This was true before you accomplished a thing for the kingdom, even while you were numbered among the sinners. You do not need to earn, achieve, or strive for God's acceptance. This is your birthright as his child.

Granted, it's not easy wrapping your head and heart around what I am saying. It has been difficult for me. I spent years working to measure up, be enough, and do great things in order to hold back God's anger and earn his love. I had bought into the belief that the starting place of discipleship was striving to be enough for God. If I'm not careful, I can wander back there.

Your first steps as a Christian were, and always will be, on the solid ground of who you are because of Jesus: loved even before you knew you were lovable, chosen even before you knew you were acceptable, empowered even before you knew you were filled with the same power that raised Christ Jesus from the dead. That is who you are, and believing that is the foundation of your relationship with Jesus.

A Journey Christian

Think of the Christian life as a great journey that began the day you accepted Christ. On that first day, you were placed on a path that stretches far into the future. Everyone who walks on this path is a child of God, regardless of whether he or she has traveled the way of Christ for years or have barely taken his or her first steps. Even those who have reached their final and eternal destination are no more or no less a child of God than you.

You may think, "I have way more leftover baggage from my old life than those who are walking ahead of me. They know more, have done more, make fewer mistakes, and seem closer to Jesus than I am." All of that may be true, but I assure you none of that changes the fact that you are on the same footing they are, a secure child of God. They are loved, chosen, and empowered, and you are loved, chosen, and empowered.

When you were placed on this path, you were given everything you needed to successfully make the journey (Eph. 1:3). On your very first day as a Christian, you received the same blessings, promises, power, and connections with Jesus that the most seasoned and mature Christian has as he or she walks with Christ. The only difference may be that some people ahead of you better understand what has been freely given to them and as a result are more secure in their relationship with God. Maybe they have grown to trust what God has declared to be true and are less inclined to believe the lies of the evil one. They may know how to rely on the Holy Spirit's help as they walk the difficult and trying sections of the journey.

"Box" Christians strive to achieve the blessings of God and work hard to earn his gifts and promises. They remain anxious about whether they are in or out with God, hoping that somehow they can prove they are enough. You, however, now know you are a child of God and have received everything you need for life and godliness. You are loved. You are chosen. You are empowered. That is your confidence.

I encourage you to be a "journey" Christian, not a "box" Christian. From this day forward, welcome self-discovery, every day allowing the Lord to unleash the wonder within you, teaching you how to live out of what is true in Christ. Remember: this is not about what you need to be. You are on the path because of who you are: a cherished and gifted child of God. You may have a great deal to learn, and you will probably fall and skin your knees along the way, even make some big mistakes. But there is no question about who you are—the real deal, God's beloved, a brilliant work of art from the Father's hand.

I want to reaffirm something God's Word says about you that I hope will bring you satisfaction and joy:

"Congratulations. You have been accepted!"

EXPERIENTIAL

The primary purpose of any spiritual exercise, including this one, is to raise your awareness to the presence of the Lord. *Understanding* theological truths and concepts is important, but deep change occurs when you are positioned to *experience* what God has declared to be true. Whether that experience comes as a gentle whisper or a great wind is determined by the Lord. Your part involves opening your senses, surrendering to the moment, and welcoming the Holy Spirit's help. When you do, faith becomes sight.

Prepare yourself. Turn away from the noise that usually surrounds you and move to engage RING with the Lord. Enter your safe place with expectation, inviting the Holy Spirit to empower this moment for a holy encounter with the One who lavishly loves you. Remember that deep breathing raises awareness as it releases tension in your body. Stay present in this moment, for it holds a treasure designed just for you.

Remain in the Light

Move toward the following scripture as though it holds a special message for you from your heavenly Father. Remember that God has breathed life into his Word. Stay open. Move slowly. Look for the hidden gifts. Approach reading these passages as a sacred encounter, anticipating that God has something he wants to say to you.

There are two passages, both revealing truths about the gifts God has placed in your life. When you see one of those gifts, stop and gaze at the wonder his Word is revealing to you.

O Lord our God, the majesty and glory of your name fills all the earth and overflows the heavens. You have taught the little children to praise you perfectly. May their example shame and silence your enemies!

When I look up into the night skies and see the work of your fingers—the moon and the stars you have made—I cannot understand how you can bother with mere puny man, to pay any attention to him!

And yet you have made him only a little lower than the angels and placed a crown of glory and honor upon his head.

You have put him in charge of everything you made; everything is put under his authority: all sheep and oxen, and wild animals too, the birds and fish, and all the life in the sea. O Jehovah, our Lord, the majesty and glory of your name fills the earth. (Ps. 8 TLB)

To the church of God in Corinth, to those sanctified in Christ Jesus and called to be his holy people, together with all those everywhere who call on the name of our Lord Jesus Christ—their Lord and ours:

Grace and peace to you from God our Father and the Lord Jesus Christ.

I always thank my God for you because of his grace given you in Christ Jesus. For in him you have been enriched in every way—with all kinds of speech and with all knowledge—God thus confirming our testimony about Christ among you. Therefore you do not lack any spiritual gift as you eagerly wait for our Lord Jesus Christ to be revealed. He will also keep you firm to the end, so that you will be blameless on the day of our Lord Jesus Christ. God is faithful, who has called you into fellowship with his Son, Jesus Christ our Lord. (1 Cor. 1:2–9)

Imagine Prophetically

These passages are filled with truth about the endowments God has placed in your life. Ask the Holy Spirit to help you picture these specific truths about you. Again, invite the Holy Spirit to use your imagination, helping you see and experience what God is saying about you.

From Psalm 8

- God pays attention to you.
- He places a crown of glory and honor on your head.
- He has placed you in charge.
- He has given you authority.

From 1 Corinthians 1

- You are called.
- You are set apart.
- You are holy.
- You have been enriched in every way.
- You do not lack spiritual gifts.
- You will be held firm to the end.
- You will be found blameless on that day.
- You are in fellowship with Jesus Christ.

Notice

Pay attention to what God's Word is saying about you. This is who you are, not who you need to become. These truths represent only a part of what God's lavish grace has placed in your life. It is ample evidence that, because of Christ, you are a wonder.

- Notice the breadth and depth of what God has done for you.
- Pay attention to your feelings as you consider all this.
- Did you notice distractions as you contemplated these Scriptures? What were they?
- Were there old recordings running through your mind contradicting what God declared to be true? What were those old messages?
- Of all these truths, which one went deepest into your heart? Why?

Give Thanks

Sit down and write a thank-you letter to God; then read it aloud to someone you trust.

10

GIFTS THAT
KEEP ON TAKING

Dad lost a piece of himself when Mom died, which was understandable given that they had been married for seventy-two years. Her death left a huge hole in his life, and it was sad watching him try to fill it. I visited him several times a week at the assisted living facility and usually found him asleep in his overstuffed lift chair with the television set tuned to an old western.

I stepped into his apartment one day and heard a noise in the spare room. I found Dad awkwardly balancing himself on his walker, sifting through a box he had somehow dragged from the closet. Preoccupied, he didn't respond when I greeted him.

"Hey, Dad. What are you up to?" He turned, looked at me, then went right back to rummaging through the box.

"Dad, how are you?" Again, no response. I stepped closer and gently turned him toward me. "What are you looking for, Dad?"

He lifted his head, stared into my eyes for a long moment, then said, "I don't remember."

I chuckled, which he didn't appreciate.

"There's something in this box I want, but I don't remember what it is."

"Do you want some help?"

"If I don't know what I'm looking for, how are you going to help?" That made a lot of sense and was even a bit philosophical.

"Dad, if you don't know what you're looking for, why do you keep looking? Let's go watch TV."

"Leave me alone. I'll know what I want once I find it."

I Didn't Know It Was Jesus

Years earlier, a guy made a similar comment, but it wasn't about looking for something in an old box. It was about searching his whole life for anything that might fill the emptiness that nagged at his soul every day. After coming to Christ, he remarked, "Jesus was what I didn't know I was looking for all that time."

This man had lived a rugged life, and the road map etched on his face told the story. He had waded through a lot of heartache and loss over the years and had the look of a person who spent his share of time on the down and out. A couple of failed marriages, grown kids who had little time for him, two trips to rehab, and a history of lost jobs were part of the debris left in his wake. He had made a lot of choices that went bad, with little to celebrate and much to regret.

Beneath his many failures and poor choices were legitimate longings that he tried to fill in illegitimate ways. He wanted love the same as we all do, as well as acceptance, security, and probably significance. Somehow, in his twisted way, Satan got involved in the guy's life, made false promises, and lured him to choose unwisely, over and over again.

It wasn't that he connected with only bad people. They just weren't big enough to fill the huge hole he had in his life. When the pain became too great, and his choices let him down, he tried something else. Like all false fillings, nothing worked, nothing lasted. In the end, his attachments drained him of life, and he turned to whatever painkiller half-promised to work. He made too many investments in gifts that keep on taking.

When he at last crashed at rock bottom, he turned to Christ and was saved. *Saved* is the perfect word to describe what occurred in his life. God plucked him from the path beelining toward destruction and miraculously placed him in the way of Jesus. God gave him a long bath in grace and deposited all the blessings he would need for a journey of self-discovery.

Beneath the scars and road burn from his past life was a masterpiece of God's transforming love. With the help of some new friends and the Holy Spirit, he began walking the Way. The future held challenges, but he was with Jesus now, filled with the gift who could satisfy what he didn't know he had wanted all along.

Idols of the Heart

God is jealous for you—not *of* you but *for* you. He wants to bless you and keep you and brag in heaven that you belong to him. He wants to shower you with grace and give you his peace (Num. 6:24–26). God is a devoted Father and has placed you securely in his heart, and in turn, he wants to make your heart his home. He asks that you love him with all your heart, mind, soul, and strength (Matt. 23:37), knowing that he alone can satisfy your deepest desires in life.

You want to be loved, to belong, to be secure, to have purpose, and to be significant, as does every other human being. These longings have been stirring in you since the moment you were conceived, desires that are meant to woo you into God's embrace.

God wants to connect with you at the place of your longings and knows what you want in life, even if you don't.

Herein lies the problem. The world wants you to look to anything but God to fill those desires. Like a carnival hawker, the world cries out that it knows exactly what you need, and with the help of the evil one, it puts a false shine on whatever it peddles, appealing directly to your deepest appetites. The world and the devil aim precisely at legitimate human desires, hoping you will invest in "gifts" that in the end only *take*, never give.

The children of Israel bought what the evil one was selling, and God was not pleased (Ezek. 14). They were filling up their hearts with false idols instead of seeking the presence of God, and as a result God was jealous.

False loves destroy and never build, take and never give, drain and never fill. God loves you too much to sit back and watch you be destroyed by gifts that keep on taking. You are meant to be attached to him as the source of your deepest desires, and God will do what is necessary to free your heart from any false fillings.

It pleases God that you desire love and significance. He affirms your longing for acceptance and security and wants you to seek purpose for your life. He is concerned, though, when you turn toward false loves for satisfaction and not him. As Augustine said, "Keep seeking what you are seeking. Just stop seeking it where you are seeking it." Remember: Jesus is what you didn't know you were looking for all the time.

When Good Becomes Bad

Blaise Pascal wrote:

> What else does this craving, and this helplessness, proclaim but that there was once in man a true happiness,

of which all that now remains is the empty print and trace? This he tries in vain to fill with everything around him, seeking in things that are not there the help he cannot find in those that are, though none can help, since this infinite abyss can be filled only with an infinite and immutable object; in other words by God himself. God alone is man's true good.

Pascal was right. Nothing created, regardless of how big and beautiful, will ever fill the void in our hearts. We surely do try to fill that empty space with anything and everything that might promise satisfaction. The restlessness created by unmet desire begs for our attention, and we end up with a heart full of idols that demand our energy and drain our lives.

We would be wrong to think that idols of the heart are fundamentally evil. Most people try to satisfy core longings with good things. They look to their jobs, their relationships, their possessions, their appearance, even their bank accounts as the source of satisfaction. There is nothing inherently evil about any of these, and when properly placed, each can be a resource God uses to bless them. But there is nothing permanent or secure about any of these things. They will never satisfy the deepest cry of the human heart.

Can a person lose a job? Of course. So if a person believes their job is the source of significance, and invests their hope for fulfillment there, they are building on a risky foundation. People can lose their bank accounts, their relationships, their appearance, even all their possessions. Looking to any of these to satisfy deep longings creates nothing but insecurity. People end up hypervigilant. Anxiety, not rest, characterizes the life of someone attached to anything other than God for their deepest longings.

Many times I have made a statement that makes people very uncomfortable. "The best thing I ever did for my marriage was detach from my wife." People squirm in their seats, glance at my wife to see her reaction, shake their heads, and stare at me as if I were stupid to say something like that out loud. Regardless, it's true. Detaching from Cheryl was one of the best things that ever happened to our relationship.

I came into marriage with tremendous insecurity. It may have been masked behind a projected image of strength and competency, but I was an anxious guy still restless for love, significance, and security. Trauma in my childhood left ugly scars and unprocessed wounds, which did not vanish the day I came to Christ. Fundamental questions about my identity nagged at me, including "Am I lovable?" "Am I safe?" "Am I significant?" "Do I matter?" I didn't know that only God could meet those longings, so I was a prime candidate for any lure Satan threw my way.

I didn't sit down and write a list of expectations of Cheryl or talk to her about all my emotional needs. I figured she loved me, I loved her, and everything would work out for the best. So we got married, and I unknowingly took the baggage of the past along on our honeymoon. I didn't tell Cheryl she was responsible to make me feel loved, secure, and significant, but I subconsciously measured her commitment to me by that standard. When I struggled, I let her know that it was at least in part because of what she was doing or not doing.

If Cheryl would just get on board with my needs, all would be well. I never considered that my longings were not her responsibility. After all, she was my wife. So when unmet longings made me restless, the problem surely had something to do with Cheryl. I tried to put Cheryl into the God-shaped void in my heart and then judged her for not being big enough to fill it.

As you can imagine, this didn't fare well for our marriage. I had attached my longings to Cheryl in ways that were unhealthy for us both, and by doing that, I drained life from our relationship. No matter what Cheryl did or tried to do, it was never going to be enough to meet my longings for security, love, and significance. I had made her an idol.

Dealing with this was not easy. I needed the Holy Spirit to help me recognize what my unmet core longings were in the first place, and then understand that God alone could satisfy them. That took time. Second, I needed to see that I had attached legitimate longings to Cheryl in illegitimate ways, and while she could be a resource God might use to show me love, she was not the source of love for my life. Only God could fill that desire.

Third, I needed to see specific ways in which I placed that burden on Cheryl, discovering patterns of misplaced expectations that drained our relationship. Once again, that took time and a great deal of help from the Holy Spirit, as well as many conversations with Cheryl. Finally, I had to have the courage to detach. I had to take that giant umbilical cord that ran from my heart to Cheryl and attach it to the heart of God. Only God will ultimately meet the deep longings of my life.

Since then, two things have happened. I have become more aware of when internal restlessness signals an unmet longing. When I take the time to notice, I am able to turn to the Lord, tell him what I am struggling with, and ask for help trusting that he can provide. Also, my marriage was revolutionized. Attached to God, Cheryl and I are finding that being together *brings* life, not *drains* life. God's presence, where we once inappropriately placed each other, has brought an overflow of love, security, and significance to our relationship.

Which leads to an important question: Are there idols in your heart? God is jealous for you and longs to meet the deepest longings of your life. He will not share that space with illegitimate and false fillings. He wants *all* of you, not part of you, and will not share your heart with your career, your degrees, your possessions, your abilities, or your relationships.

When your heart is God's home, he is able to bring an overflow to your life. The process of detaching from false loves and attaching to God begins when you ask the Holy Spirit to help you discern the deepest cry of your heart.

What Do You Want?

One day when Jesus was with John the Baptist, two of John's disciples heard John call Jesus "The Lamb of God." They decided to leave John and follow Jesus. Seeing them walking behind, Jesus asked, "What do you want?" (John 1:35–39). They answered that they wanted to know where Jesus was staying, to which the Lord replied, "Come . . . and you will see" (John 1:39).

At first glance it appears that Jesus simply wanted to know why they were following him. I suggest that a closer look may reveal hidden treasures particularly relevant to the discussion of human core longings.

Obviously, these two men were spiritually hungry, given they were disciples of John the Baptist. What drove that hunger? What need was being touched by following John? Was it related to a deep core longing? Rather suddenly, they choose to investigate Jesus, whom John earlier called "God's Chosen One," the One able to baptize people with the Holy Spirit (John 1:32–34).

Why did they choose to leave John and follow Jesus? Did they even know why? Could it be that Jesus wanted them to look beneath their choice to find what drove that decision in the first place? Is it possible that Jesus was not asking the question for his benefit, but for theirs?

Even the wording of their response seems layered. The English translation states they wanted to know where the Lord was *staying* (John 1:38). The Greek word translated "staying," *meneis,* is later translated "remain" in the Lord's teaching about vines and branches (John 15). There, the Lord told his followers that remaining connected to him was the only way they could bear fruit and find joy. The concept of remaining is not about a physical location but about drawing life and meaning from a heart-to-heart connection with Jesus.

I'm not suggesting these two men were aware of what Jesus was asking. I do think Jesus was pushing them to look deeply at what was driving their interest in him. Instead of telling them where he was staying, Jesus invited them to "come" and "see," wanting them to experience where the Lord "remained." Could it be that Jesus wanted them to see his daily heart-to-heart, connection with the Father? Maybe he wanted them to discover that God was the source of life for Jesus—and could be for them as well.

The choices we make in life, from relationships to occupations to where we live to purchases and to countless other decisions can, if we look closely, lead us to the unmet core longings we are desperate to fill. That was true in my marriage, and equally true in countless decisions I have made, even when the decisions seemed random and benign. The decisions we make can signal how we are trying to fill longings, often in illegitimate ways.

Desire drives choices, and those choices are like crumbs along a path. If you follow them, they can lead you to what you really want in life if you have the courage to stop and look. I know Jesus wants to help you detach from anything and everything that is an idol of the heart, that drains life rather than gives life. You may have thought your choices would provide what you needed for a fulfilled life. Yet time and experience should convince you that sometimes what you received were gifts that keep on taking.

Pascale was right: only God in Christ can fill the vacuum in your life. Created things will never do.

EXPERIENTIAL

The Lord knows you have chosen to follow him, and as he did with two men long ago, he invites you to experience his presence, to stay with him, to learn from him. Choose to set aside some time to go to your sacred space. Prepare to meet him there. Take a few deep breaths and invite the Holy Spirit to help you encounter the Lord.

Remain in the Light

Invite the Holy Spirit to help you slowly read and contemplate the following Scripture. Remember to look closely, not simply at what is written but at the meaning that may lie beneath the words you read.

> The next day John saw Jesus coming toward him and said, "Look, the Lamb of God, who takes away the sin of the world! This is the one I meant when I said, 'A man who comes after me has surpassed me because he was before me.' I myself did not know him, but the reason I came baptizing with water was that he might be revealed to Israel."
>
> Then John gave this testimony: "I saw the Spirit come down from heaven as a dove and remain on him. And I myself did not know him, but the one who sent

me to baptize with water told me, 'The man on whom you see the Spirit come down and remain is the one who will baptize with the Holy Spirit.' I have seen and I testify that this is God's Chosen One."

The next day John was there again with two of his disciples. When he saw Jesus passing by, he said, "Look, the Lamb of God!"

When the two disciples heard him say this, they followed Jesus. Turning around, Jesus saw them following and asked, "What do you want?"

They said, "Rabbi" (which means "Teacher"), "where are you staying?"

"Come," he replied, "and you will see."

So they went and saw where he was staying, and they spent that day with him. It was about four in the afternoon. (John 1:29–39)

Imagine Prophetically

I hope to lead you in a specific experience of prophetic imagination. In your quiet and sacred space, take several deep breaths and let them out slowly.

- As you breathe, invite the Holy Spirit to be with you, giving him permission to use your imagination as a way to encounter the Lord.
- Imagine yourself in a safe, quiet setting, sitting quietly in worshipful expectation. Spend several long moments at rest there.
- With your eyes closed and heart open, imagine Jesus standing in front of you. His arms are outstretched

toward you, the expression on his face communicating love and acceptance.

- Pay attention to your feelings and body response as you see Jesus reaching toward you with love.
- Now hear Jesus ask you this question: "What are you seeking?"

Don't answer with the first thing that comes to your mind. Allow the question to take you deeper, looking to the unmet core longing of your life. What is the desire that drives many of your choices, the desire that can be met only in him?

In a single sentence, tell Jesus what you want, the longing of your heart. Is it security? To know you are loved? Significance? Purpose? Acceptance? To be understood? Tell him in a single breath.

Wait for the Lord's response.

Now carry this prayer with you and offer it to Jesus each time deep restlessness calls for your attention.

Notice

Spend time journaling your experience. The following questions may help you center.

- Did you experience distractions as you began this exercise? What were they and how did you handle them?
- What did you feel as Jesus stood lovingly before you?
- What did you notice about the Lord's body posture toward you?
- What was your body response?
- What did you say when the Lord asked, "What are you seeking?"

- Was your answer linked to a deeper core longing? If so, which longing?
- How have your life choices signaled deeper desires?
- Where have you tried to fill legitimate longings in illegitimate ways?
- Have you experienced "gifts that keep on taking"? If so, what were they and how have they drained life from you?
- Is there a specific place in your life in which the Lord is asking you to detach, and then attach to him alone? Where? What will be your first steps?

Give Thanks

The psalmist writes,

> At last I shall be fully satisfied; I will praise you with great joy. (Ps. 63:5 TLB)

The Lord extends his arms toward you in love. He wants to fill the deepest longings of your life, to be the gift that keeps on giving. You will be fully satisfied. What is your song of thanks and praise to the Lord today?

11

WOUNDS, LIES, AND TOO MUCH LOSS

W hy do Christians get stuck? If we have everything we need for life and godliness, why do we get bogged down in our faith? Why do we often feel alone on the journey, even with the Holy Spirit living inside us? If our identity is secure, and we are loved, chosen, and empowered, why do we struggle with so much doubt? What causes us to fill unmet longings with false loves instead of turning to the Lord?

I've been there. Every Christian I know has been there. You've probably been there. We start making good progress as believers, we want to go deeper with the Lord, we begin to connect with brothers and sisters of the faith, we decide to start going the extra mile in our spiritual lives, and then bam!—we hit a wall. No matter how hard we try, we can't get over it, under it, around or through it. We pray, we read our Bibles, we go to church, we worship, and yet we stay stuck? Why?

We all hit a few dry spots in our Christian life. We wander away and get trapped in sin. We let our guard down and the evil one does his best to steal, kill, and destroy. At times, the dark harmony of voices gets to us and we start believing we don't measure up. We stop turning to God with our deep longings and get hooked by Satan's lures. Something as obvious as neglecting time with the Lord can stall our spiritual growth. In these cases, basic spiritual disciplines and the encouragement of fellow believers usually help recharge our spiritual lives.

Something else is happening when you start spiraling into a place of despair and experience disconnection from the Lord. When your efforts to pray more, read more, and do more bring frustration, when dysfunctional behaviors seem to control your life, when your descent accelerates no matter what you do, deeper issues are begging for your attention. It could be that unhealed emotional wounds are keeping you in bondage. When that's true, the only way forward is to ask the Lord to help you look back.

The unhealed and unprocessed past does not stay in the past, regardless of how hard you try to forget. You might fight to keep bad memories from coming to mind—repressing, denying, anesthetizing, and rationalizing—but it seldom works and will not last. In the end, you exhaust yourself playing emotional Whac-a-Mole, hopelessly trying to keep the past from raising its ugly head. You'll never win at that game. As sure as the sun rises and sets, the unhealed past will leak into the present and compromise your well-being.

Every emotional rupture demands repair, whether it happened yesterday or fifty years ago. The unaddressed past reaches into the future, and all you see is what happened yesterday. Henri Nouwen wrote, "By cutting off our past we paralyze our future: forgetting the evil behind us, we evoke the evil in front of us." Sometimes the wall you are facing today was actually constructed a long time ago.

Why the Past Is Always Present

Lori was quiet, always smiling, and often at the church doing odds and ends. She was the first to help a neighbor or friend in need, the picture of a supportive pastor's wife. People in the congregation applauded her gifts of hospitality and servanthood, and while her husband thrived up front, Lori found satisfaction in less visible roles. Or so it seemed to everyone.

Lori lived with secrets. Behind her bubbly image was a boiling caldron of anger and hate. She resented being a pastor's wife, a role she despised but felt obligated to play. Lori was afraid to voice discontent to her husband but regularly lashed out with passive-aggressive behavior, aimed with laser precision.

Lori obsessively picked at her skin, small wounds kept hidden beneath her clothing. Like the relief valve on a steam engine, picking was a dysfunctional way for Lori to release the chronic self-contempt that consumed her thinking. She seethed over people's expectations, yet had no idea what she wanted to do or who she wanted to be. Lori lacked confidence and refused to step out in self-discovery, yet hated the fact that she allowed people to define her role in life.

Was Lori a Christian? Absolutely. Lori received lavish grace the day she came to faith in Christ. She was a loved and chosen child of God and had everything she needed to successfully walk the way of Christ. But Lori was stuck neck deep in the past, trapped by emotional wounds that happened long before she met the Lord. She was in a prison not of her own making, and it was ruining her relationship with her husband, her family, and her Lord.

Lori was raised by a raging father and a deceitful mother. Her dad ruled with an iron fist, barking orders like a marine drill sergeant, laced with foul language and contempt. Lori grew up terrified of him. Her brothers would occasionally talk back when he raged, but Lori said nothing. She cowered like a helpless child as her dad walked all over her.

Lori was responsible for general housework as a young girl. Her mother taught school, so Lori had to cook, clean, fold clothes, and clean up after everyone. One evening, while sitting at the dining room table doing homework, she asked her dad for help. He told her to go to the kitchen and do the dishes. He made the decision that her mother would do the homework for Lori because she could do it faster and better. That wounded Lori and became a defining moment in her life. Lori believed she wasn't smart, so she needed to keep her mouth shut and do what she was told.

After years of insecurity and self-contempt, things began caving in around Lori. Her marriage was crumbling, she felt like a fake in her relationship with God, and she had no idea what she wanted out of life. Pretending was killing her. Lori needed help but did not know that any hope for a better future would require her to meet Jesus in her painful past.

Regardless of Lori's age, there was a frightened child inside of her begging to be safe. There was also a teenage girl within her who believed she wasn't smart enough to try new things. A loud voice kept warning Lori to keep her mouth shut and do what she was told.

Emotional wounds do not instantly heal the day you accept Christ. Healing memories, like other aspects of Christian growth, are part of the journey to freedom. It takes time, and you need help along the way. Jesus cares about that pain and wants to use his wounds as a source of healing for your wounds. Jesus is tender toward the broken: "a bruised reed he will not break, and a smoldering wick he will not snuff out" (Isa. 42:3).

Stages of Brokenness

While the details of Lori's story are different from yours, there is a noticeable pattern of cause and effect to emotional brokenness. Unrepaired emotional wounds cause people to believe things about themselves and about God that are simply false. Those false beliefs nag at them and generate chronic negative feelings, which bring a great deal of pain to their lives. People end up trying to kill that pain in ways that do far more harm than good.

You can see the pattern of cause and effect emerge in Lori's story when, like peeling an onion, you look at her life.

Dysfunctional Behaviors: Lori would hide, pretend to be someone she was not, keep her mouth shut, act out toward her husband, and punish herself through picking at her skin. Beneath those behaviors were chronic negative emotions.

Chronic Negative Emotions: Lori struggled with anger, resentment, fear, insecurity, and anxiety. Those feelings were generated by false beliefs she held about herself and her world.

False Beliefs: Regardless of what God declared to be true about Lori, early wounds caused her to believe that she was not safe, not smart, inadequate, and unable to get it right. These false beliefs were shaped by emotional wounds, painful events that Lori experienced as a child.

Emotional Wounds: Lori's father was controlling, loud, demanding, and demeaning. Her mother did not challenge his abuse and used passive-aggressive behavior to get her way. This wounded Lori, and, unrepaired, those wounds crippled her adult life.

Early brokenness kept Lori in bondage to self-contempt, even though she was filled with gifts and treasures her loving heavenly Father poured into her.

I have experienced this pattern of brokenness in my life and have sat with hundreds of brothers and sisters who experienced the same. Like Lori, we all received lavish grace, everything we needed for life and godliness, and yet we're stuck. Gratefully, Jesus is able to step across time. When he does, healing and freedom are possible. Broken Christians can move beyond surviving to thriving. It took many years, but Lori finally decided to make that journey with the Lord.

The Healing Journey

Lori came to the end of herself, needing to find freedom. As important as prayer, Scripture reading, worship, and other Christian disciplines are, she needed more than traditional spiritual exercises. Lori needed to experience a deep emotional healing of toxic wounds that had hindered her growth for years. She decided to reach out to a Christian prayer counselor, but it was Jesus who took her by the hand.

Talking about what happened in her past was not enough to free Lori. The emotional wounds had taken root through an experience and now Lori needed a new experience with Jesus in order to be healed. With her prayer counselor's help, Lori journeyed back in time to the day she sat at her parent's dining room table and asked her dad for help.

Lori allowed the Holy Spirit to access her imagination, enabling her to be a mental time traveler, back to that moment long ago. She was able to see herself as a teenage girl, sitting at the table struggling with her homework. Fear rushed to the surface when she heard her dad say, "Go to the kitchen and do the dishes. Your mother will do your homework. She'll do it faster and better." Shame began to suffocate Lori as it had those many years before.

Lori began weeping uncontrollably. Grief spilled out like an overturned water bucket as sadness tore at her soul. Through tears she cried, "I'm nothing. I can't do it right. I'm so lost." Her prayer counselor stayed present to the pain, assuring Lori that God was with her in that awful moment.

Lori's prayer counselor asked her to invite Jesus into the picture. Lori was able to see Jesus in the kitchen with her as she obediently washed the dishes. He approached her tenderly and slowly drew her into his embrace, allowing her to cry into his chest. Jesus said he was sorry that her dad had treated her that way. It was wrong for him to be mean with her and make her so afraid. As Jesus spoke, Lori wept. The Lord's presence surrounded Lori like a soft cloud, and she began to feel the burden lift.

Jesus told Lori about things he liked about her. He said that she had a heart full of love yet to be released and a tenderness that would bring healing to many people. Lori was special, wanted, and filled with gifts that he would help her develop. The Lord promised Lori that she was always safe with him. He would help her step into a new way of living, to find her place in the world, and be free.

These were not words read from a page by Lori's prayer counselor. This was a transforming experience with Jesus. The toxic memory filled with shame became a new memory of Christ's love and devotion. There was more healing yet to come for Lori, additional memories that needed to be redeemed by the Lord. On that day, however, Jesus began tearing down the wall that kept Lori in bondage, enabling her to take the first steps into her identity as a beloved child of God.

Your Healing Journey

Possibly wounds of the past are compromising your walk with Jesus. Yesterday may be robbing you of today, keeping you from experiencing the awakening the Lord intends for you. There is good news. Jesus cares deeply about your entire story and wants to bring every moment of your life, past as well as present, into his embrace. Remember: "a bruised reed he will not break, and a smoldering wick he will not snuff out." Jesus is waiting to meet you in the broken places of your life.

Your journey of healing will begin when you ask the Holy Spirit for help. Don't take a pick and shovel to your past, trying to find memories that are causing you to struggle. Give the Holy Spirit permission to uncover your unprocessed wounds. Let it happen in his time and in his way. The Lord is far more interested in your well-being than you are. Take the courageous first step and tell the Lord you are stuck. Be honest, and when you are, Jesus will meet you in your unprocessed past.

Remember: emotional healing is a journey. There will be moments when you sense a deep release, when prison doors swing wide open. Even when that happens, you still must learn to walk out your healing by replacing old ways of thinking, behaving, and living. The Holy Spirit will help you each step along the way. Learn to rely on him, and as you do, new awakenings will open the way to endless possibilities. You will begin experiencing the abundant life Christ promised (John 10:10).

If you're struggling, find a gifted caregiver who is willing to make the healing journey with you. I would have never found freedom without the help of skilled people who understood the process of emotional healing. I have spent two decades teaching mature Christian men and women a model of deep healing I call "formational prayer." Thousands have been helped, experiencing healing moments with Christ. Information about my organization, Healing Care Ministries, is available at the end of this book.

Jesus does not want you to walk this out by yourself. Link up with other "journey" Christians who will help your spiritual development. Awakening happens best "where two or three are gathered" in Christ's name. Find a community of believers who speak grace fluently, for whom love and encouragement are their native tongue.

The Father longs to be gracious to you. Allow Jesus to take you by the hand and lead you to freedom. There is no wall he cannot pull down, no prison door he cannot take down, no night so dark he cannot find you, not pit so deep he cannot free you. Jesus does it all by the power of his love.

EXPERIENTIAL

Dark forces align against your desire for self-discovery, hoping you will never realize that you bear the image of God. They want you blinded to the full potential of your life. Combat them by intentionally setting aside time to meet the Lord. While the experience of awakening is a work of the Holy Spirit, positioning yourself is your responsibility. Step away from the noise, and make room for Jesus.

Remain in the Light

Slowly read this psalm of David. Pay attention to words and phrases encouraging you to meet the Lord in difficult places within your life.

The LORD is my light and my salvation—
so why should I be afraid?

The Lord is my fortress, protecting me from danger,
    so why should I tremble?
When evil people come to devour me,
    when my enemies and foes attack me,
    they will stumble and fall.
Though a mighty army surrounds me,
    my heart will not be afraid.
Even if I am attacked,
    I will remain confident.
The one thing I ask of the Lord—
    the thing I seek most—
is to live in the house of the Lord all the days of my life,
    delighting in the Lord's perfections
    and meditating in his Temple.
For he will conceal me there when troubles come;
    he will hide me in his sanctuary.
    He will place me out of reach on a high rock.
Then I will hold my head high
    above my enemies who surround me.
At his sanctuary I will offer sacrifices with shouts of joy,
    singing and praising the Lord with music.
Hear me as I pray, O Lord.
    Be merciful and answer me!
My heart has heard you say, "Come and talk with me."
    And my heart responds, "Lord, I am coming."
    (Ps. 27:1–8 NLT)

Imagine Prophetically

I am introducing you to a spiritual exercise called "The Safe Place."
Its purpose, like those of all spiritual exercises, is to raise awareness

to the presence of God. In this case the focus is upon developing an internal place of safety where you can meet the Lord, engaging not only your mind but your body and senses as well.

This exercise will position you to meet the Lord, enabling you to see and hear him better. It is critical that you feel safe with him on your healing journey, and this will help. Remember: this may take time, so move slowly and repeat the exercise.

- Sit quietly in a comfortable position.
- Take several deep breaths, letting them out slowly.
- Begin to whisper words of thanks and praise to the Lord.
- After a few moments, invite the Holy Spirit to sanctify your imagination.
- Ask the Spirit to create within your mind a safe place where you can meet the Lord. It may be an imaginary place or somewhere you have been, like a cabin, beach, or favorite spot along a quiet stream.
- Rest there for as long as you like. Allow all your senses to be present, enjoying everything you experience in your imagined surroundings. Pay attention to what you are seeing, hearing, sensing, and feeling.
- If you experience some dissonance or distraction, ask the Holy Spirit to take it away in the name of Jesus.
- When ready, invite the Lord to join you in that place. If that frightens you, ask him to come as the Lamb, or to simply allow you to feel his presence.
- Once there, notice the warmth of his love. Let it soak into your being. If you are allowing Christ to be with you,

notice his posture, eyes, and extended arms. Draw close to him if you desire.

- When ready, tell Jesus how you feel about him. Then ask how he feels about you. He may respond with words or actions. Either way, experience his acceptance and delight.
- If you are ready to conclude the exercise, simply spend a few moments in thanks and praise.
- Take a few deep breaths, letting them out slowly.
- Amen.

Notice

I once heard a pastor ask God to give people eyes to see, ears to hear, and hearts to respond. That would be a great prayer to consider as you notice what God is saying to you from Psalm 27.

Having spent time in "The Safe Place" exercise, turn your attention back to Psalm 27. It may help to reread the passage.

- What thoughts arose as you read this passage?
- List the images from the psalm that help you feel safe.
- If there were only one thing you wanted to ask of the Lord, what would it be?
- Imagine you needed to process unhealed wounds of the past. What promises from this scripture would encourage you to make that journey?
- If the Lord invited you to come and talk with him, what would you say?
- Notice your feelings. What are they trying to tell you?

Give Thanks

The apostle Paul wrote, "give thanks in all circumstances; for this is God's will for you in Christ Jesus" (1 Thess. 5:18). When you notice the movement of God in your life, whether it be blessings great or small, gratitude is the proper response. Given the promises contained in Psalm 27, I suggest there are several reasons for you to be thankful today. Choose to use a song, a hymn, a prayer, or journal entry to express your heart to the Lord.

12

A HARSH GOSPEL

I learned a lesson as a child that went marrow deep: behave, or bad things will happen to you. My mother impressed that principle onto my hide on many occasions. If looks could kill, my sister and I wouldn't have made it past the third grade. Mom regularly gave us the death stare for our bad behavior. No sound evoked more terror in my soul than the silverware drawer being snatched open to retrieve the wooden spoon.

Mom was not above bringing God in on the job. Mom said God was watching when she was not and doled out punishment to rule-breakers with bolts of lightning and all-consuming fire. One of my mother's favorite Bible stories was of Elisha and the two bears that laid waste to forty-two disrespectful boys. My sister and I knew not to tick off Mom or God and never walked home from school by way of the woods—just in case! The phrase "Behave yourself" held apocalyptic implications for us both.

My grandfather added his brand of fear with a "visual" demonstration of how misbehavior causes really bad things to happen. He lost an eye in a work-related accident and wore an ocular prosthesis, better known as a "glass eye." It became a prop for his twisted brand of humor, and he used it to ignite fear in children's hearts. My cousin had a habit of picking her nose, so Grandpap said, "If you don't stop that your eye will fall out"—at which point he would place his finger into his nose, dislodge his glass eye, and let it skip across the floor. A small tribe of half-crazed kids ran screaming from the room.

His glass eye became a resource for behavior modification: "Go to bed or . . ." and out came the eyeball, "Eat your dinner or . . ." "Listen to your grandmother or . . . ." It was torture. I was amazed as a child just how many behaviors could potentially send your eyeball sailing across the living room floor. It's interesting that some of his grandchildren, me included, lived with rather serious anxiety and insecurity, especially around the thought of sudden disaster befalling them. We all knew that if you didn't behave, bad things were going to happen.

The adults thought the whole thing humorous. They would laugh at Grandpap's antics and recount tales around town of his ocular gymnastics as if they were stories from the Brothers Grimm.

It bothered me that his behavior was justified because it seemed to work. My cousin did quit picking her nose, though she soon started hiding in the closet to pull out her eye lashes. "See? It worked" became the classic ends-justifies-the-means rationale from my parents. The terrorizing of young hearts was overlooked because the kids learned to behave. I found the whole circus of the damned harsh and uncaring. We learned to walk on eggshells, fearing body parts would suddenly drop off if we failed to toe the line.

A Harsh Gospel

As a young Christian, I viewed the gospel through a distorted lens shaped by those early experiences with my mother and family.

"Do good, get good; do bad, and you'd better watch out." I had to behave to enjoy the embrace of God. Misbehaving meant sure and sudden punishment. Given the consequences were now eternal, I had to give serious attention to living right or else.

Some churches use that same lens. They mention Jesus enough to identify their perspective as Christian, but discipleship is more about behavior modification than faith in Christ. Being right with God, as they see it, requires holiness, which is illustrated by specific behaviors, not the fact that we are made holy the moment we take our first step in the way of Christ.

I'm not suggesting that people who believe or promote this paradigm of faith are bad or nonbelievers. I *am* saying, however, that this "harsh gospel" is a distortion of the good news of Christ. People encouraged to follow Christ this way seldom awaken to the wonder already present in their lives. They are blinded by performance and held in bondage to measuring up.

The harsh gospel creates anxiety. People worry about where they stand with God, feel shame because they fail, wrestle with insecurity since behavior determines acceptance, struggle with fear because judgment looms, and are exhausted, wearing themselves out trying to measure up. The harsh gospel is not an easy yoke, is not gentle, the burden is far from light, and it will never bring rest for the soul.

The harsh gospel works against much of what I am proposing in this book. It can blind you to the scandalous grace of Jesus Christ and to the wonder that God has placed into your life. While much of it sounds Christian, the subtle nuances of the harsh gospel stifle self-discovery. In the end, you will neither know yourself nor know God.

The apostle Paul wrote that a little yeast can work into the whole dough (Gal. 5:9). Even a small amount of this harsh gospel can throw you off course and things will go sideways fast. Once while working as a carpenter, I made a small mistake laying measurements for a ninety-foot-long wall we were building at a medical center. It was less than a quarter-inch error, made within the first foot. Ninety feet later, what began as an imperceptible slip-up created our own version of the Leaning Tower of Pisa. My boss was not pleased when we had to tear it down and start over!

Confusion results when Christian leaders move away from the scandalous grace of Christ and teach that acceptance is based on behavior. More importantly, it violates the offense of the cross (Gal. 5:10–12), the truth that security with God comes only through faith in Christ. Reconciliation with God does not come by adhering to rules, rituals, and religious obligations. It is important that you recognize the harsh gospel for the distortion it is.

There are six characteristics of the harsh gospel. The first two were covered in detail in previous chapters.

- The harsh gospel prioritizes who you need to be over who you are in Christ.
- The harsh gospel gives great attention to who is "in" and who is "out."
- The harsh gospel begins by sharing bad news.
- The harsh gospel emphasizes your behavior rather than Christ's behavior.
- The harsh gospel suggests that Jesus did *almost* everything you need to be secure with God, and you must do the rest.
- The harsh gospel defines "real Christians," coupling proper behavior to identity security.

Who You Need to Be over Who You Are

As stated in a previous chapter, emphasizing who a Christian needs to be, as opposed to who he or she is, as the starting place of discipleship unbiblically couples performance with identity security. It's a bad place to begin the Christian journey. The Bible is quite clear that becoming a child of God is a matter of faith, not behavior. (Gal. 3:1–6). It also teaches that a new believer receives everything he or she needs for life and godliness from day one (Eph. 1:3). Whether another person can see change in your life or not, the treasures of the kingdom abide there in abundance. They simply need to be awakened and released.

There is no external litmus test that infallibly proves to others that you are a Christian. Whether people like it or not, only God knows the state of your heart. He alone defines you as his child, regardless of what anyone may think. There are churches that may insist upon standards for belonging, usually around beliefs and behavior. However, using a religious yardstick to measure acceptability only sends folks into hiding.

Who Is In and Who Is Out

"Box" churches, as we learned previously, measure people by a list of nonnegotiables they believe are essential to the Christian life. I live in a community filled with the Amish, where beliefs and behaviors determine acceptance, down to the type of clothes they wear and the buggies they ride through the community. There is no question about who is in and who is out.

While a more extreme example, the same thing happens in more churches than some want to admit, though it may be more subtle. Whether it is a little yeast or the whole dough, "in" and "out" thinking is based on a harsh gospel that never sets people free. It only leads to a self-centered preoccupation with measuring up.

When Sharing the Good News Begins with Bad News

Many of us learned a method of sharing Christ that walked through the book of Romans, beginning with two scriptures meant to capture people's attention. It began by telling people that they were sinners and that sin has a payday, the wages being eternal death (Rom. 3:23; 6:23). Starting with that message does not fit with most people's definition of good news, regardless of what comes next. In fact, as a starting place for sharing Christ, it is neither good nor is it news. It is a harsh gospel.

If you were to read the verses that come before and after Romans 3:23, you would find that rather than bad news, it embodies a message that is nothing short of breathtaking. It says that God has made a way for all people to be at peace with him, and it has nothing to do with following the rules. People, like you and me, can be connected to the loving heart of God by believing in Jesus. It's true that everyone has messed up and sinned, equally broken and beat up. But now, through Christ and his death on the cross, we can receive the gift of salvation, all by faith in God's lavish grace (Rom. 3:21–25).

There is a true scandal to the gospel, genuinely good news. If people properly understood the message of Christ, they would find it hard to believe because it is so good. It is breathtaking.

Emphasizing Our Behavior over Christ's Behavior

When I fell in love with Cheryl, I became obsessed with her. I wanted to spend all my time with her, wanted to know everything about her, loved to look at her, be with her, smell her perfume, kiss her, and dreamed of spending my life with her. I was unqualifiedly

Cheryl-crazy. Surprisingly, my fascination with Cheryl made me want to be a better person.

That glorious obsession should pale in comparison to your love for Christ. The Holy Spirit will help you make Jesus the center of your life—living in him, rooted in him, built up in him, and strengthened in your faith in him (Col. 2:6–7). Jesus can be your true north, helping you successfully navigate the challenges of the Christian journey.

The harsh gospel keeps the spotlight on you, not Jesus. It wants you to obsess about how you are doing, your failures, your wanderings, and your misbehavior. That is spiritual navel-gazing that will get you nowhere but down.

Jesus came to earth, emptied himself of the glory he had in heaven, lived a perfect life, died on a cross, rose from the dead, and then assigned your name to that life. You have received the benefits that were due Jesus, freely given to you by grace. Amazing!

While the harsh gospel wants you preoccupied with how you are doing, the glory of the gospel shines on what Jesus did, in your name. Spend as much time as you can focusing on who Christ is, what he is like, and what he did for you. If you focus there, something wonderful will be released in you.

Jesus Did Almost Everything You Need to Be Secure

I'll admit to a strange insecurity I had when I first came to Christ. Almost every day I worried about heaven. I didn't worry about whether I was going to get there, just about whether I could stay there. I thought I would make a mistake up there and either get kicked out or spend time sitting in the corner, wherever that might be. I was sure that I couldn't maintain heavenly behavior for more than a minute or two.

One day Jesus settled the matter. He said, "Terry, you are going to get in because of me, and you will *stay* in because of me! It is not about you." That was liberating, especially since my early years of discipleship were marked by constant pressure about how I was doing, and it wasn't always a good report.

Did Jesus do everything necessary for you to be secure in your identity as a child of God? Or did Jesus do *almost* everything, and you need to make up what is lacking through good behavior? Which is it? The harsh gospel demands sin management as a requirement for your security. You must follow the rules to be safe with God.

Paul wrote that adding a single requirement, other than faith in Christ, was a perversion of the gospel (Gal. 1:6–7). It leaves people anxious, focused on themselves rather than the glory of Christ crucified. Identity security must be uncoupled from behavior. When it comes to being a secure child of God, your behavior does not matter. Only faith in Christ matters.

You have a new identity because of Christ, a new intimacy with the Holy Spirit because of Christ, and a new inheritance that will neither spoil nor fade because of Christ (Gal. 4:4–7). Is it then any wonder why you should boast only in Jesus?

The List of Dos and Don'ts for Real Christians

Cheryl and I were driving in the country when a giant billboard captured our attention. Someone spent serious money sharing a message with people who passed by. It read, "Real Christians Obey the Teachings of Christ."

There are a number of wordings that would have brought an "amen." If it had read, "Christians should obey the teachings of Christ," or "It would be smart to obey the teachings of Christ," or even "Let's all ask the Holy Spirit to help us obey the teachings of Christ." Any one of those would have been fine.

As soon as anyone links obedience to being a real Christian, it is a distortion of the gospel. It is a harsh gospel claiming that someone who struggles is not the real deal, which is ridiculous. I know real Christians who struggle with alcoholism, who speak against their neighbor, who wrestle with sexual issues, who don't read their Bibles, who fail to go to church, who are not generous, and who have divorced their spouses.

It is a harsh gospel that suggests that if you struggle you are not a real Christian. No one can live up to that. I certainly cannot. Should I be obedient? Of course. Hopefully, with the Holy Spirit's help, I will grow to live out who I really am in Christ. That is the process of spiritual formation. It is what the Lord wants to accomplish in all our lives.

You are a real Christian because you have expressed faith in Christ, because God has redeemed you by the blood of Jesus, because you have the Holy Spirit living inside. You have received a new identity, new nature, new heart, new spirit, new gifts, and a new community. You have been a real Christian since the day you became a new creation in Christ Jesus, filled with wonder and gifts freely given and yet to be discovered. You will misbehave as a real Christian, and when you do, it does not make you any less real. It makes you human and in need of Christ's help.

You must not allow the harsh gospel to take root in your life. Nothing good will ever come of it. You have been set free from the burden of measuring up, so don't allow anyone to place that ball and chain on you ever again. If you do, the spotlight will be on you and not on Jesus. Stand as far away from that as possible (Gal. 5:1–6). You are a Jesus person, so stay Christ-possessed and all will be well with your soul.

EXPERIENTIAL

Jesus waits to meet you in sacred space and sacred time. Do not simply go there—run there. The Lord of the universe, through his Holy Spirit, welcomes your presence and wants to spend concentrated time with you. Slow down, breathe deeply, meet him in the present moment, and awaken to wonder.

Remain in the Light

Contemplate the following scriptures that highlight the generosity and grace of the gospel of the kingdom.

> Therefore, since we have been made right in God's sight by faith, we have peace with God because of what Jesus Christ our Lord has done for us. Because of our faith, Christ has brought us into this place of undeserved privilege where we now stand, and we confidently and joyfully look forward to sharing God's glory. (Rom. 5:1–2 NLT)

> What actually took place is this: I tried keeping rules and working my head off to please God, and it didn't work. So I quit being a "law man" so that I could be God's man. Christ's life showed me how, and enabled me to do it. I identified myself completely with him. Indeed, I have been crucified with Christ. My ego is no longer central. It is no longer important that I appear righteous before you or have your good opinion, and I am no longer driven to impress God. Christ lives in me. The life you see me living is not "mine," but it is lived by faith in the Son of God, who loved me and gave himself

for me. I am not going to go back on that. (Gal. 2:19–21
The Message)

Imagine Prophetically

When you ask the Holy Spirit to use your imagination to help you better understand God's Word, you are integrating what he is saying at two levels: understanding and experience. Opening your senses, body awareness, spiritual sensitivity, and intuition deeply encodes God's truth into your life. Go beyond mere concepts and experience the presence of God. Invite the Holy Spirit to help you encounter the breathtaking grace of the gospel.

Reread Galatians 2:19–21 and use it as the basis of your imaginative encounter with the Holy Spirit. As always, begin by taking a few deep breaths, asking the Spirit to use your imagination in order to better embrace God's truth.

- Ask the Holy Spirit to help you see ways in which you have tried to keep rules and "work your head off" trying to please God.
- Discern, with his help, the difference between being a "law person" and "God's person." What does that look like for you?
- What words would you use to tell people that you now completely identify with Christ?
- Invite the Holy Spirit to help you see what it was like to live by other people's opinions of your Christian walk.
- How were you driven to impress God?

- What does it mean that Christ is alive in you? Ask the Holy Spirit to help you see and understand that great truth.
- Invite Jesus to live his life through you, instead of your trying to live your life for him.

Notice

- What feelings are you experiencing?
- What did the Holy Spirit show you about the difference between being a "law person" and "God's person"?
- What does being free from other people's opinions look like for you?
- Quiet your heart and notice that in this moment, Jesus is alive in you. Will this make a difference in the way you walk his path? If so, how?
- You are stepping away from the expectations of a harsh gospel. Make a declaration that from this day forward you will not go back.

Give Thanks

In 1 Corinthians 1:31 Paul quoted the prophet Jeremiah, who said, "Let the one who boasts boast in the Lord."

What is your boast about Jesus? Let that be your act of gratitude today, boasting about the breathtaking gospel of Jesus Christ.

13

SIN MATTERS

The look on his face spelled trouble. I had been talking about Christian identity, the fact that we are secure, not because of our behavior but because of faith in Christ. As I did, I noticed an older gentleman squirming in his third-row seat, intensity building like a rubber band stretched to the breaking point.

Something I said bothered him, and he was determined to let me know about it. The man raised his hand, arm waving like an elementary school kid desperate to visit the restroom. Words were about to spill out of his mouth like soda from a bottle shaken a bit too long.

"Dr. Wardle, I have a question, and I'm not the only one. Folks here are upset. You stood there and said that sin doesn't matter. You handed everyone a license to do whatever we well please, telling us that God is okay with that. Dr. Wardle, you're soft on sin, and you're wrong."

Bypassing the fact that this was an accusation and not a question, I responded. "No, that's not what I said."

You would have thought I had said his mother wore combat boots. He stood, waving his finger at me. "Yes, you did. You did.

Everyone here heard it." He turned his head and looked around the room. "Didn't he? He said it, and we all heard him."

I paused, took a deep breath, and glanced across the crowd. This wasn't the first time someone had gotten angry with me during a seminar, especially when I discuss God's extravagant grace. It throws some people off, particularly "box" Christians. Most believers would say righteousness comes by faith alone; but deep inside, they still believe behavior, good or bad, determines their standing with God.

"Actually, what I said was that behavior doesn't matter, when . . ."

The man stopped me midsentence, pointing to the participants, and said, "See? He said it again. You heard it. 'Sin doesn't matter.'"

"People do not become Christians because they keep the rules. Do you agree?" I was looking for a nod, but nothing.

"We became God's children through faith in Jesus. That's it. From the day Jesus takes us into his heart, we belong to God. We don't earn it or deserve it or achieve it. It's is a gift of grace. Like the prodigal son, you are his child when you're with him, when you wander from him, and when you crawl back home covered in mud. You are secure sons and daughters, and behavior doesn't change that."

A woman's hand went up. "What you are saying just sounds too good to be true. It sure isn't what I've grown up believing. Part of me wants to believe you, but there is another part . . . this is scary. I've spent my life measuring up and I don't want God mad at me."

"I get it. All I can say is that grace is that good. Becoming a child of God is God's gift to you, all because of Jesus."

There was mostly silence in the room, as if they were staring at a prison door suddenly flung wide open, wondering if it were safe to step into freedom.

"Well, if it *is* true," another participant asked, "what would keep people from sinning all they want?"

"I would hope two things," I said. "First, we should stop sinning because it is our worshipful response to God's grace. Think of all he has done for you. Obeying him is one way of saying thanks— to show your gratitude by living as his holy people.

"You don't have to behave to be secure with God, but you *should* behave because you are secure with God. It is your worshipful response to his love. Second, we need to stop sinning because it hurts us and hurts other people as well."

"So sin matters, right?" the first man asked.

I smiled, nodded my head, and said, "It does. Sin matters."

A Worshipful Response

How should you respond to God's extravagant grace? There are three options, and at one time or another I have waffled back and forth between each. First you could think, "This grace stuff sounds great. However, I don't want to take a chance and get on God's wrong side. So just to be sure, tell me the rules so I can stay secure with him." Just a friendly warning: this response is an invitation to some serious exhaustion.

You could go in the opposite direction. You might see grace as a get-out-of-jail-free card, a license to do whatever you please. When someone challenges your bad behavior, tell him or her, "Grace has me covered," or "I'm not into judgment." If that doesn't work, "Grace is hard-wired into me." You might want to know this response comes with a lot of pain and brokenness.

You could make a more balanced response to grace. God's gifts are lavish, his love unconditional, and the inheritance of faith beyond description. You realize that you have received everything you need for life and godliness on day one, are loved, chosen, and empowered. You are a grateful, secure child of God, with nothing to earn, achieve, or add to that security. So you decide that your behavior will reflect who you are in Christ. You choose, with the Spirit's help, to walk the way of love the way Jesus walked the way (1 Cor. 14:1).

Think about this. You have peace with God through Christ (Rom. 5:1–2), eternal life as a gift from Jesus (Rom. 6:23), you stand free from all condemnation because of Jesus (Rom. 8:1), you are more than a conqueror through Jesus (Rom. 8:37), you are righteous by faith in Jesus (Rom. 9:30–32), and you are part of a remnant chosen by grace, not good behavior (Rom. 11:5). All is yours because of the lavish grace of God, poured out through the Holy Spirit since you gave your heart to Christ.

The apostle Paul challenged Christians to live in worshipful response to God's great love. He told the Roman believers to make everyday activities an offering to God, whether sleeping, eating, working, or just hanging out with other people. He wanted them to reflect the grace poured out freely in their hearts and display the virtues and values of God's good kingdom in daily life. This lifestyle was to be an act of gratitude for all the Father had done for them in sending Jesus (Rom. 12:1–3).

Living by the virtues and values of the kingdom is your response to God's love as well. That's why you should stop sinning. Consider all God has done, and then live every day as a reflection of the grace he has so generously poured into your life.

You are a masterpiece of God's creativity, a living image-bearer filled with wonder and brilliance. Let your ordinary life be an extraordinary reflection of who you are in Jesus. Remember: the Holy Spirit will help you all along the way.

Sin Really Does Matter

When anyone claims emphasizing grace makes you soft on sin, point to the cross of Christ. Jesus shed his blood so that you could be free. There was not a single thing you could do about sin on your own. What obeying the law was powerless to do, Jesus did by hanging on Calvary's tree. His death made you right with God (Rom. 4:25). Only his unblemished blood could cleanse and free you from sin's tyranny (Heb. 9:14).

The condition of sin goes far too deep for human behavior to set it right. Only the sacrifice of the Son of God could loose sin's chains around your heart. Jesus canceled the debt that condemned you, and he did it at the cross (Col. 2:14). You are secure in Christ, God's beloved child, which is reason enough to shout, "Thank you, Jesus! I am forgiven and I am free!"

It may help for me to define what I mean by sin, specifically as it relates to your life as a believer. I am not suggesting it involves a list of do's and don'ts. The definition is more fundamental than that. Sin is failing to live out who you are in Christ.

You have been given a new nature, a new heart, a new spirit, a new identity, and a new intimacy with God through the indwelling presence of the Holy Spirit. You are a new creation, filled with gifts and treasures from the hand of God, including the ability to live by the virtues and values of the kingdom.

Granted, you need the Holy Spirit to help you walk out this new life. That is what the process of sanctification is all about. Don't let the word *sanctification* intimidate you. It simply means "the Holy Spirit empowered process of living out who you now are in Christ."

The Spirit will reveal where you are falling short, then use his power to help you step away from sin and back onto the way of Christ. Your part is to surrender to that process. Sanctification takes time. It is a long journey of personal growth. You will stumble along the way and possibly turn back to old behaviors. When that happens, talk to the Lord about it. Jesus will forgive and cleanse you, put you back on your feet, and get you walking again on the way of love (1 John 1:9).

Be careful, though. Don't get the impression that sinning doesn't matter. Sin hurts you even as a Christian, particularly in the following ways.

- Sin can blind you to who you are in Christ.
- Sin can break your fellowship with the Father.
- Sin brings harm to you and others.
- Sin can enslave you.
- Sin can bring you shame.

Sin Can Blind You to Who You Are in Christ

Let's go back to the illustration of the pig who was turned into an eagle. If Jesus turned the pig into an eagle, and that eagle kept rolling around in a pig sty, the eagle could lose touch with who he really was. If the eagle ate like a pig, hung out with pigs, smelled like a pig, and acted like a pig, he might simply conclude he *was* a pig, even though he was an eagle the whole time. Covered with mud, he couldn't get off the ground no matter how hard he tried. He might conclude that he was nothing more than a smelly old pig in the first place.

Sin, failing to live out of who you are in Christ, gives you a distorted view of yourself. You could easily conclude that you are what you do, when that is simply not true. You are not your greed, or meanness, or sexual addition, or selfishness, or any other sin you might be caught in. You are a child of God to the core.

You are a new creation who might not have learned how to live as the new creation you are. Sin will weigh you down. It will keep you from soaring in your new life. Sin is serious business.

That being true, sinning is not a statement about your identity or the inherent brilliance in your life. You are amazing because of Christ. Let the Holy Spirit help you, every day, walk the way of Jesus the way Jesus walked the way.

Sin Can Break Your Fellowship with the Father

The theologian Clark Pinnock once wrote, "Spirit is leading us to union—to transforming, personal, intimate relationship with the Triune God." Union with God is at the heart of why Jesus came to earth. He came to provide a way for you to enjoy close fellowship with your Father. Union, intimate fellowship with God, is where the Christian journey is taking you.

The story of the prodigal son, from Luke 15, comes back into focus. You have already discovered that the son was secure with the father—a son when he was at home, a son when he wandered away, and a son when he came limping back. The son's identity was never compromised because of his sin. However, his fellowship with the father was compromised. Straying from home meant stepping away from the father's provision and care.

Sin leads you away from the Father's house of love and becomes a barrier to intimate fellowship with him. It is not that the Father turns away from you. If the story of the prodigal son tells you anything, it is that the Father is always searching, always looking, always hoping for your return. Repentance is about your returning to the house of love where God's embrace brings satisfaction and rest.

Sin is wandering away from love, and sin matters. When you sin, seek the Spirit's help and make the journey home where the party awaits.

Sin Brings Harm to You and Others

One sentence says it all. You reap what you sow (Gal. 6:7). You may no longer be in bondage to the law of sin and death, but sin still matters. You can hurt yourself and hurt others when you choose to step away from the path of Christ.

I have a friend who decided to spend the evening drinking. Later, quite inebriated, she drove her car to the store and on the way wrecked into a guard rail. Gratefully, no one was injured. She was arrested for drunk driving, lost her driver's license for six months, and as a result lost her job. She actually blamed God for the mess—he should have stopped her from driving that night. If he was really a God of grace, he wouldn't have punished her by getting her arrested, which cost her a job.

Losing her license and her job had nothing to do with God's punishment. It was the direct consequence of her bad behavior. This was about a choice, not a judgment pronounced from the Father. Sin is like that.

Serious harm can happen when you decide to wander from the house of love. It has happened to me, and it will happen to you. Even as God's cherished child, filled with wonder and brilliance, sin can hurt you and other people. You need the Holy Spirit. Ask him every day to keep you on the way of Jesus.

Sin Can Enslave You

Satan doesn't begin by tempting you to eat the whole apple. A first bite will do. That is how Jason became trapped in sexual addiction. It began when, as an impressionable preteen, he stumbled across his father's magazines hidden in the basement workshop. Jason began to sneak down there whenever he could to look at pictures, and what he saw aroused feelings that, at least for a while, soothed his feelings of insecurity.

Over time, the magazines lost their glow, so once in college, Jason moved on to movies and videos. What started as an occasional choice soon became a pattern. First weekends, then evenings, and eventually pornography dominated his life. Jason married, believing things would settle since he could enjoy a sexual relationship with his wife. His addiction continued, however, and soon began to destroy his marriage.

The descent into bondage begins with a single choice, and soon choices become habits, which can become bondage. Before you know it, what seemed at first harmless leaves you out of control. When part of your life is not occupied by Jesus, it becomes ground for the evil one to claim. You must be well armed against the devil and fully aware that sin matters.

You are an amazing icon of God himself, your whole being an instrument of righteousness. Don't give Satan a foothold. If you stumble, remember that the Father is quick to forgive, cleanse, and reclaim what belongs to him (1 John 1:9).

Sin Can Bring You Shame

It was day three of a seminar I was doing in Colorado Springs. The theme was emotional healing, and as I sat in morning worship, the Holy Spirit impressed upon me that people were battling shame. I felt led to offer an opportunity for people to receive prayer. I anticipated that a few folks would respond, and then we would move on to the topic for the day.

I was shocked by the response. Close to seventy people came forward, many weeping as the Lord cleansed them from shame.

For well over two hours, I saw men and women who had been harassed by feelings of self-contempt, unworthiness, and judgment set free by the transforming power of Christ.

Shame is like an invisible, yet highly perceptible pond scum that you wear because of past failures, wounds, and false beliefs. Christians are especially vulnerable to shame, given the evil one points constantly at sin, past and present. He wants you to obsess over your mistakes, wallowing in regret and self-abuse rather than running to the One who promises forgiveness and cleansing. Yes, sin happens, sin blinds, sin hurts, and sin brings shame, yet the power of Christ can always set you free. Sin matters, but the grace of Christ always matters more.

EXPERIENTIAL

As you move toward your safe place, think about the posture of the prodigal's father in the Lord's parable (Luke 15:11–32). Always generous, always watching, always forgiving, always blessing. This is precisely how the Father looks at you. Meet him in this moment like a child running home to the Father's tender love. Remember: deep breathing, quiet, and present-moment awareness will help you encounter his presence.

Remain in the Light

Your reading for today comes from selected verses of Psalm 139. Move slowly, allowing the Word of God to come alive for you. Ask the Holy Spirit to make these verses especially relevant to the topic of this chapter. Allow the promise of God's care and attention to motivate you to pray those final words: "Search me, O God."

O LORD, you have examined my heart
    and know everything about me.
You know when I sit down or stand up.
    You know my thoughts even when I'm far away.
You see me when I travel
    and when I rest at home.
    You know everything I do.

I can never escape from your Spirit!
    I can never get away from your presence!
If I go up to heaven, you are there;
    if I go down to the grave, you are there.
If I ride the wings of the morning,
    if I dwell by the farthest oceans,
even there your hand will guide me,
    and your strength will support me.

You made all the delicate, inner parts of my body
    and knit me together in my mother's womb.
Thank you for making me so wonderfully complex!
    Your workmanship is marvelous—how well I
know it.

How precious are your thoughts about me, O God.
    They cannot be numbered!
I can't even count them;
    they outnumber the grains of sand!
And when I wake up,
    you are still with me!

Search me, O God, and know my heart;
   test me and know my anxious thoughts.
Point out anything in me that offends you,
   and lead me along the path of everlasting life.
   (Ps. 139:1–3, 7–10, 13–14, 17–18, 23–24 NLT)

Imagine Prophetically

Invite the Holy Spirit to use your imagination, engaging your senses, body, and spiritual intuition to engage this text. Move through each section of the psalm slowly, experiencing the nearness of God and his tender attention to your life.

- Ask the Lord to give you a picture of his constant attention, watching over your every move and thought.
- Ask the Holy Spirit to give you a picture of the Lord taking your hand and guiding you along the path.
- Ask the Lord what it means that you have been fearfully and wonderfully made. Again, try to picture that.
- Give the Holy Spirit permission to fill your mind with thoughts of God.
- Are you willing to allow the Lord to search your thoughts? What will he find?
- Is there anything about your thoughts you need to confess?

Notice

- What thoughts came to your mind as you considered that God knows you, sees you, and is ever present with you?
- What feelings arise when you consider his attention?

- Scripture says that God takes you by the hand. What does that mean to you?
- What does being fearfully and wonderfully made mean to you?
- Which of your thoughts about God inspire you? Bring you peace? Help you in difficult times?
- Review the feelings that arose when you considered the Lord searching your heart.
- What did he find that you need to confess? Anything to surrender? Something you need to change?

Give Thanks

Review what you experienced in this exercise. List the insights and inspirations you received from the Lord, thanking him for each. Choose one and share it with a friend.

SAYING YES TO AN EVEN GREATER AWAKENING

14

AWAKENING TO THE HOLY SPIRIT

Our farm is a magical place to our grandchildren. It represents freedom, providing opportunities for excitement that their more domestic existence in the suburbs doesn't offer. The kids arrive, put on farm boots, overalls, and hats they wouldn't dare wear in public—then off they go to explore.

They love the barn, constructed of giant beams hand-hewn from timbers harvested on our land in the mid-nineteenth century. Names and dates have been carved into wooden posts, telling a story time refuses to forget. Every fall the hay mow becomes a castle of straw, begging the kids to imagine a time and place long gone to most people.

Critters of all kinds pass through, giving the kids an education that books could never offer. This spring they ran screaming when seven skunk kits walked through the front yard on their way to the woods. Spring fawns are their favorite; mangy coyotes their least.

Treasure hunting is the farm's greatest allure. The kids have unearthed fossils from the stream, arrowheads in plowed fields, and an ancient celt left centuries ago by a Native American. They have dug up old horseshoes, chisels, pieces of chain, worn-out tools over one hundred years old, and even a coin or two. These worthless pieces of rusted metal are priceless treasures, displayed for everyone to enjoy.

On the other side of the eastern border stand four cherry trees whose branches sag under the weight of ripe cherries. The trees are not ours to harvest. While I'm sure there has been some sneaking, the rule is—if you don't own it, you don't pick it.

Then something happened. I needed to put up a new fence to keep the goats in, so I had the land surveyed. Much to my surprise, we own well beyond the fence, including all the cherry trees. That old beat-up fence was lying all the time, telling us to stay on our side, when for years sweet cherries belonged to us, waiting to be enjoyed.

Beyond What We Can Ask or Think

Do you want to go on great adventures, uncover hidden gems, and find things you never knew were yours? Do you long to find that special place where you are welcome, wanted, and free to be you? Doesn't the idea of hidden treasure stir something deep within your soul? Wouldn't you love to pick fruit that tastes like heaven itself?

No, I'm not still talking about our farm. I'm talking about your life in the Holy Spirit as he awakens you to the wonder of the kingdom of God. Whatever our farm offers, it pales in comparison to what the Holy Spirit wants to bring to your life.

The Holy Spirit has given you a lifetime membership in the kingdom of God. He wants to lead you on an adventure where priceless treasures are yours for the asking. He longs to entice you beyond mundane domesticity to the richness of life as a child of the King. Jesus has made the Holy Spirit your personal guide on this adventure, your helper, your teacher, and your brillianteer.

Awakening to the Holy Spirit turns ordinary people into extraordinary children of God. Earthbound people become servants of a heavenly kingdom; sleepy Christians awaken to the wonder that abides within the human heart. Awakening to the Spirit causes eyes to see, ears to hear, and hearts to respond to the movement of God. The adventure of a lifetime begins when you cry out for awakening.

The Holy Spirit makes some people nervous. Jesus did say the Spirit is undeniable, uncontrollable, unexplainable, and unpredictable (John 3:8). Even the metaphors the Bible uses for the Holy Spirit can induce some anxiety; fire, wind, and rushing water. Considering the Holy Spirit brought the universe into being, hovered over creation, and raised Christ from the dead with incomparable power, encountering him can be intimidating.

The Bible does also refer to the Holy Spirit as a dove. People like that metaphor because it makes them feel safe, as if the Spirit is small, soft, harmless, even controllable. We welcome the Holy Spirit to come to us as a dove as long as he doesn't land on someone and leave a mess.

Father Benedict Groeschel referred to the Holy Spirit as "God in his outrageous mode." That is a far cry from the Spirit as a gentle spiritual butler, dispensing demitasse-sized servings of living water to the mildly disinterested. Groeschel's definition sparks images of open fire hydrants blasting geysers of water on the unsuspecting, sending people slipping and sliding into the streets like the crowd at Pentecost.

The Celts named the Holy Spirit "the Wild Goose." They knew the Holy Spirit could never be domesticated or tamed, refusing to bend to human will or serve people's selfish desires. "The Wild

Goose" disrupts the comfortable and comforts the broken, all on his own terms. There is an element of danger and risk to the Holy Spirit, especially if you decide to chase "the Wild Goose," and even more so if "the Wild Goose" decides to chase you.

The Holy Spirit does move gently at times. I have experienced his tenderness when healing emotional wounds, his comfort in times of heartache, his peace when anxieties swirl, and his rest when I've worn myself out trying to measure up. The Holy Spirit has guided me like a mother would a small child, patient, encouraging, pouring hope into my despairing heart.

There is always an element of mystery to the Holy Spirit, the sense that no formula applies to his coming or his going. The Holy Spirit can be gloriously outrageous, coming like a mighty wind, like tongues of fire, shaking houses off their foundations, causing the alive to fall dead and the dead to new life. He can also speak with a quiet whisper and move across your life like a soft summer breeze. No matter how you encounter the Holy Spirit, be prepared for an awakening that will change your life forever.

Like Christmas Morning

Cheryl and I love it when our son or one of our daughters invites us to spend Christmas with him or her. There is something magical about Christmas morning, especially with little ones. They awaken full of anticipation and joy, running to the tree to see what gifts have serendipitously arrived with their names attached. Wrapping paper is torn away in nanoseconds and boxes thrown open to reveal hidden treasures belonging just to them. The kids hold up each present for Grandma and Papa to see, watching for the sparkle in our eyes that says, "Wow—that's a great gift you have!"

Awakening to the Holy Spirit is like that—only his gifts await new every morning. When he opens your eyes to the unfolding of the kingdom, life presents possibilities that are, dare I say, outrageous. The Holy Spirit places a deposit of heaven into your daily life, the treasure of his presence and the promise of things yet to come. These gifts are yours, freely given, able to unleash wonder inside you, and in turn service to the world around you. All this and more are yours for the taking.

Sadly, many Christians are barely awake, weighed down trying to measure up, exhausted from the bondage of performance. When difficulties come, which they do for everyone, they end up facing trial and temptation in their own strength, unaware of how the Spirit longs to help them. The Christian journey is exciting, but not without dark valleys and desolate terrain. Jesus never intended that you face this alone, so he sent the Holy Spirit to be your guide and helper.

The awakening of the Holy Spirit begins when you realize that *God gives you the Holy Spirit not because you behave but because you believe in Christ* (Gal. 3:1–6). The infilling of the Holy Spirit is a gift of grace. It is unearned and undeserved, yet generously poured out upon you from the moment you invite Christ into your heart.

I remember years ago uttering the simplest prayer of faith, and what followed has forever changed my life. God opened the floodgates of heaven, and the Holy Spirit began flowing in my life like a deep river (John 7:38–39). This awakening begins by faith when you place your trust in the lavish outpouring of love expressed through the life, death, and resurrection of Jesus.

Jesus told Nicodemus that he had to be born again to see and enter the kingdom of God (John 3:1–8). This initially confused Nicodemus until Jesus clarified that he was speaking of a spiritual birth. Awakening was at the core of what Jesus was describing, telling Nicodemus that it is impossible to see the movement of the kingdom unless you are spiritually awake.

As mentioned earlier, what Jesus said to Nicodemus harkened back to something recorded in the book of Ezekiel. Hardened hearts and dead spirits can never move in the flow of the kingdom or perceive what God is up to in the world. Faith in Christ, however, brings the spiritual awakening that was promised centuries ago. *The new birth in the Holy Spirit enables you to see the kingdom at work and empowers you to participate in the movement of God that is changing lives.*

You host a beloved guest in your heart, and part of his ministry is confirming that you are a secure child of God. Scripture says that *God sent the Holy Spirit into your heart to call out "Abba, Father,"* over and over, assuring you that you belong to him (Gal. 4:6). *Abba* is a term of endearment and intimacy, used by Jesus and Paul to signify your enduring connection with God. A more modern rendering would read, "The Holy Spirit repeatedly whispers, 'He's your daddy.'"

I drove my elementary school children to school every day when we lived in Palo Cedro, California. Day after day, as they exited the vehicle and began walking toward the building, I would shout, "Remember who you belong to!" I wanted my kids to know there was a safety net under them because we were connected as family. God wants so much more for you to know the same! You are not an orphan. You are a child of God, and frankly, the Holy Spirit is not going to let you forget.

There is, by the way, something that my son, oldest daughter, and I have in common. We all have a symbol of the Holy Spirit tattooed on our bodies. I tried to get my wife and youngest to join us, but needles are a bit much for them, though I haven't given up trying to convince them.

Did you know that you are marked as part of the family of God? The Bible says that *God has set his seal of ownership on you, which is the promised Holy Spirit* (2 Cor. 1:22; Eph. 1:13–14.) God doesn't want anyone confused about whom you belong to. You are God's child and he has set his seal on you to prove it. There will be a great "sortin' out" day in the future, and the Lord does not want to lose you in the crowd. So he has placed his spiritual stamp upon you, which is the Holy Spirit.

How does knowing you are sealed by the Holy Spirit affect your sense of security with God? I would think it would help you stand rock solid, even when the storm rages out of control. Add to that the fact that *God has given you the Holy Spirit as a down payment of things to come.* Every experience you have of the Holy Spirit is simply a first taste of what will be yours when you arrive in the kingdom. Have you ever been overwhelmed by the Spirit's presence, seen a healing, or experienced a miracle of God? There's still more. In fact, if you listen, you may hear the Spirit whisper, "You ain't seen nothin' yet!"

You Ain't Seen Nothin' Yet!

There is Christmas morning excitement when you awaken to the many gifts the Holy Spirit has freely given you by faith. *Part of being God's child includes experiencing the sanctifying work of the Holy Spirit* (1 Pet. 1:2). The word that frightens many believers is actually a promise meant to bring you great hope. At its root, *sanctify* means "to be set apart." God has made you special, you are one of a kind, and the Holy Spirit wants to help you live out of the uniqueness God has placed in your life.

Walking the way of Christ can be beyond tough. It can be impossible. I have a natural tendency to bend away from the Lord and reengage old habits and bad attitudes. Thankfully, the Holy

Spirit has always been there, convicting me when I stray and, when I surrender, getting me back on the right path. He is there to do the same for you. Never forget that you have been given an amazing promise by God. He started a good work in you the day you came to Christ, and he is going to finish it (Phil. 1:6). The Holy Spirit, your beloved quest, is right there to see that it happens.

The Holy Spirit does some of his best work when you are struggling with weakness. Did you know that *the Spirit prays for you when things get tough*? He is one of your two great intercessors, Jesus being the other (Rom. 8:26–27). The Bible says the Holy Spirit prays in ways you can neither hear nor understand, asking the Lord to help you stay faithful to God's will for your life. There are times when I get quiet and ask the Spirit to let me in on what he is praying. I'm not saying I always hear correctly, but the thought that the Holy Spirit prays for me brings hope and strength to my life.

Jesus said, "It is best for you that I go away, because if I don't, the Advocate won't come. If I do go away, then I will send him to you (John 16:7 NLT). My initial thought upon reading that passage was "I'd rather have Jesus." How could it be any better than being with Jesus all the time? That is until I began awakening to what the Holy Spirit brings to the Christian life. The unfolding of his gifts is endless, and no matter how much I begin to see and experience his presence, there is always more.

Any fear that awakening to the Holy Spirit will diminish attention to Christ is put to rest by Jesus himself. He said the Holy Spirit would glorify Jesus, essentially keeping the light right on Jesus all the time. The Holy Spirit highlights everything Jesus has said and done, teaching the Lord's followers to walk in the truth Jesus gave them. The bottom line is this: *The more you awaken to the Holy Spirit, the more you will fall in love with Jesus.* Your beloved guest loves to talk about Jesus, so you never need fear that you are over-emphasizing the Holy Spirit in your life. Being filled with the Holy Spirit will make you Christ-possessed.

One of the phrases I cherish from my grandchildren is "Do it again, Papa." Whether it involves hayrides behind the tractor, riding down the hill on a sled, throwing them into the air, or rolling across the floor tickling them, I seldom weary of "Do it again." Did you know that you get to say "Do it again" to the Holy Spirit? It's written in the Bible. *You get to ask to be filled with his presence again and again and again* (Eph. 5:18). Being filled with the Holy Spirit is not a one-time experience, nor does it come in "one size fits all" experiences.

Whenever you need strength as you serve the Lord, you get to pray your own version of "Do it again." Twice Jesus said that the Father loves to give the Spirit and give him without limit (Luke 11:13; John 3:34). That amazes me, especially in a "little dab will do you" world. Beginning with your first steps as a Christian, you are an empowered child of God, and the Holy Spirit wants to release that power in you over and over again. Awakening is the pathway to increasingly formative experiences with your beloved guest, and according to the Bible, you get to seek his infilling as much as you need, as often as you want—and then some.

There is one more very important truth about your life in the Spirit. *It is possible to receive the Holy Spirit and then not walk in the Spirit* (Gal. 5:25). Given what we have just discussed about the wonderful Holy Spirit, that seems unlikely, though it happens far more that you might believe. There are believers who barely recognize the presence of their beloved guest, trying to live the Christian life in their own strength. Their hearts are right, but their blindness to the Holy Spirit is crippling.

You are cherished. God is for you, not against you. He has deposited everything you need to walk the way of Christ Jesus successfully. But all of that will be as not unless you say no to achievement and yes to awakening in the Holy Spirit. The Holy Spirit longs to answer your cry for awakening. I can't offer you a formula or a surefire prayer that always works. I do know this: Jesus promised that his Father gives the Spirit without limit. The Holy Spirit is closer to you than your hands and your feet, with you in this present moment. Tell the Holy Spirit what you want. If you do, you'll never go on a wild goose chase, because "the Wild Goose" will be chasing you.

EXPERIENTIAL

Consider asking a friend or two to pray for you as you engage in this experiential. Let them know that the topic is awakening to the Holy Spirit, and ask them to pray for your deeper understanding and experience of his presence. Set aside ample time to engage with the Lord, quieting your heart and mind to encounter God in this present moment.

Remain in the Light

The Scripture reading comes from the book of Acts, often called "the Acts of the Holy Spirit." Invite the Holy Spirit to help you encounter him as you read these two passages.

After his suffering, he presented himself to them and gave many convincing proofs that he was alive. He appeared to them over a period of forty days and spoke about the kingdom of God. On one occasion, while he was eating with them, he gave them this command:

"Do not leave Jerusalem, but wait for the gift my Father
promised, which you have heard me speak about. For
John baptized with water, but in a few days you will be
baptized with the Holy Spirit."

Then they gathered around him and asked him,
"Lord, are you at this time going to restore the kingdom
to Israel?"

He said to them: "It is not for you to know the times
or dates the Father has set by his own authority. But
you will receive power when the Holy Spirit comes on
you; and you will be my witnesses in Jerusalem, and
in all Judea and Samaria, and to the ends of the earth."
(Acts 1:3–8)

While Apollos was in Corinth, Paul traveled through
Turkey and arrived in Ephesus, where he found several
disciples. "Did you receive the Holy Spirit when you
believed?" he asked them.

"No," they replied, "we don't know what you mean.
What is the Holy Spirit?"

"Then what beliefs did you acknowledge at your baptism?" he asked.

And they replied, "What John the Baptist taught."

Then Paul pointed out to them that John's baptism
was to demonstrate a desire to turn from sin to God
and that those receiving his baptism must then go on to
believe in Jesus, the one John said would come later.

As soon as they heard this, they were baptized in
the name of the Lord Jesus. Then, when Paul laid his

hands upon their heads, the Holy Spirit came on them, and they spoke in other languages and prophesied. (Acts 19:1–6 TLB)

Imagine Prophetically

Ignatius encouraged believers to enter a story in the Bible with their imaginations, as if they were there at the time. I encourage you to be fully present as you allow the Holy Spirit to make you a mental time traveler, going back to the day of the Lord's ascension and Paul's encounter with believers in Ephesus.

- Stand with the disciples and hear Jesus promise that you will be baptized not many days from now.
- Hear him say that the baptism of the Holy Spirit will make you a witness for him.
- Listen to Paul's questioning of the people in Ephesus regarding the Holy Spirit.
- Watch them be baptized in the name of Jesus, and be present as Paul lays hands upon them to be filled with the Holy Spirit.

Notice

- What feelings arose in you when Jesus talked about the coming of the Holy Spirit?
- Did anything stir in you when Jesus said, "You will be baptized with the Holy Spirit not many days from now"? Is that something you long for?
- Paul told the Ephesians that there was more for them than simply believing what John the Baptist taught. Did

you have the sense there was more for you as well? What is that *more*?

- The Ephesians were filled with the Holy Spirit as Paul laid hands on them, and they then manifested gifts of the Spirit. What gifts may the Holy Spirit want to release in you?
- Are you ready to ask the Holy Spirit for a fresh awakening? If so, even the simplest prayer in faith is welcomed by him.

Give Thanks

What is your prayer today? Before seeking a greater awakening, spend some time thanking the Lord for what he has already done in your life.

15

AWAKENING TO YOUR TRUE IDENTITY

Here's a question: If life with the Holy Spirit is like Christmas morning, which gift should you open first? That's easy. Open the one marked *identity*. Identity security, the fact that you are a child of God, should be the first thing you learn about being a new creation in Christ Jesus.

Identity provides you with a rock-solid footing for life. If you know who you are in Christ and build on the fact that you are a child of the King, unimaginable possibilities open before you. Identity in Christ can free you from the burden of achieving, allowing you to rest securely in the arms of God as a cherished member of his eternal family.

Did you ever dream of being someone else as a kid? I sure did. When tensions became unbearable at home and I was suffocating in my own angst, my imagination took me to a time and place where I was safe and, of course, very brave. I had done it all as a kid, with courage and flair—pirate, knight, soldier, sailor, professional athlete, fighter pilot, and, of course, a cowboy driving a herd across the West.

For at least a few moments, I was freed from paralyzing fear and the ugly truth that I was considered a weenie, arms covered in eczema and afraid of the dark. Imagination allowed me to travel the globe and do things I dare not try in real life. After watching Errol Flynn in *The Prince and the Pauper,* I dreamed of being discovered to be a long-lost European prince. I imagined playing in the schoolyard at Gastonville Elementary School when suddenly multiple limousines pull up beside me. Men in black suits and bowler hats, accompanied by soldiers in formal military attire, bow slightly before me and say, "Your highness."

Of course, sooner rather than later, I would be jerked back to reality. Darkness would fall, night terrors would return, and I would be alone to face the reality of just being me. Maybe this is why I found such wonder and freedom when I discovered that I really *am* a child of the King—a dream came true for me, and it is no less true for you.

Does knowing who you are in Christ make a difference in the way you live? Without question. To begin with, it impacts your self-esteem and self-worth, which affects the way you relate to other people. You no longer need to compromise who you are to be accepted by others.

When you are secure in your identity as God's beloved, you are able to invest your life in what brings you fulfillment and joy. As Frederick Buchner once remarked, you will live where your deepest gladness meets the world's need. You learn to live without inhibition, regardless of how others judge or evaluate you.

You will gain confidence when you realize you are a secure child of God. You can stop waiting for people to say you are a somebody, since Jesus has already given you all the "somebody-ness" you need. No more scanning the crowd for the noticing wink or accepting nod, crumbs of praise you previously deemed necessary to bring meaning to your life.

When you were locked in achievement, you had to prove your maturity by how you behaved, what you believed, and the way you served. Now that your identity is based on being a child of God, maturity is about union with God. You can experience intimacy and fellowship with the Father, approaching him as "Abba," transformed by the promise that his face shines on you every day.

Identity security is your eternal inheritance as God's child, a rock-solid foundation upon which you can, with the Holy Spirit's help, build your unique and amazing life. You have had a secure identity since the day you came to Christ. There is, however, a question to consider: Have you actually awakened to the fact that your identity is "child of God?"

Identity Matters

I was introduced to Howard Thurman in the early 1990s, a decade after he passed into the presence of the Lord. I was in the early stages of depression, and my good friend and doctor suggested I read Thurman. Howard Thurman's wisdom has helped me for over thirty years, particularly his classic book *Jesus and the Disinherited*.

Howard Thurman was an African American theologian and educator who played a prominent role in the civil rights movement, influencing Martin Luther King's theology of radical nonviolence. Thurman was named one of the fifty most important African American figures in history, a global religious icon who influenced countless men and women on the journey to God's embrace. His insights on human dignity and worth stand out to this day.

Howard Thurman once wrote, "The awareness of being a child of God tends to stabilize the ego and results in new courage, fearlessness, and power. I have seen it happen again and again."[1] Notice that it is not being a child of God that brings courage, but *being aware* that you are a child of God. Awareness, the fruit of awakening, makes the difference.

Howard Thurman's words are particularly empowering when you consider the context of his early life. He was raised in the Deep South, where the "white and black worlds were separated by a wall of quiet hostility and overt suspicion."[2] He regularly faced the sting of racism and marginalization growing up in Florida, where, at the time, the iron fist of Jim Crow came down on African Americans systemically.

Thurman was taught to have confidence in his God-given worth and dignity. Whenever oppression weighed heavily upon him, his grandmother would inspire him with a story from her life as a slave. He wrote,

> Once or twice a year, the slave master would permit a slave preacher from a neighboring plantation to come over to preach to the slaves. The slave preacher followed a long tradition, which has hovered over the style of certain black preachers even to the present time. It is to bring the sermon to a grand climax by a dramatization of the crucifixion and resurrection of Jesus. . . . At the end, he would be exhausted, but his congregation would be uplifted and sustained with courage to withstand the difficulties of the week to come. When the slave preacher told the Calvary narrative to my grandmother and the other slaves, it had the same effect on them as it would later have on their descendants. But this preacher, when he had finished, would pause, his eyes scrutinizing

every face in the congregation, and then he would tell
them . . . "You are not slaves! You are God's children!"

When my grandmother got to that part of the story,
there would be a slight stiffening in her spine as we
sucked in our breath. When she finished, our spirits
were restored.[3]

Confidence in being a child of God was marrow deep for Howard
Thurman, giving him strength to reject the backhand of discrimina-
tion and racism. He traveled the globe helping the disenfranchised
draw courage from the grace of God as full members of his kingdom.

Investing in Identity Security

Years ago, my wife and I were in a period of transition and the bulk
of our possessions were stored in a semitrailer on a property we
had purchased for a retreat center. Cheryl sent me on a mission
to dig through the trailer and find some clothes for the kids. As I
did, I ran across a box of keepsakes.

I decided to spend some time traveling down memory lane
and hauled two boxes of trophies, college yearbooks, and awards
outside to rummage through. The longer I looked, the sadder I
became. There was a time when I needed those awards to prove
my worth, and now they were yesterday's news packed away in
dusty boxes lying in the dirt at my feet. Worst of all, I realized that
achievement earned me a trip to the psychiatric hospital. Through
the unfocused blur of tears, things became clear. I had to awaken
to who I am in Christ.

You are a child of God. You have an incredible inheritance from
God that will never spoil or fade. Awareness of your identity, as
Thurman wrote, will instill courage and strength in your life—so
needed in a world that tells you to achieve and measure up. Now

is the time to build upon that solid rock. Here are some building blocks that might serve you well.

Spend more time listening to the voice in your heart than you do the voices in your head. A single statement can define a person's life. For most of us, things have been said that pull us toward self-rejection and contempt. Negative messages play like a continual audio loop in our minds, first spoken by people we esteemed. Now it is our own voices we hear, parroting remarks that we wish were never spoken but somehow we believe are true.

I've had my own battles with voices. Being called a "nervous child" and a "weenie" didn't serve me well when I was a traumatized kid, but it stuck. I may not use those exact words, but the voices sound much the same. One day while struggling, I stood at the fence looking at the goats feeding in the pasture. I was engaging in my daily dose of self-abuse when this thought crossed my mind: "How many times would I need to call a goat a 'horse' for it to become a horse?"

Seems silly, doesn't it? There are no words, regardless of how many times they are said, that can change identity. Why, then, do you believe those voices, as though they had the power to define who you are? You are defined by the voice in your heart, which every day whispers, "Abba, Father." Jesus has graced you with three great gifts: identity, intimacy, and an inheritance that will never spoil nor fade (1 Peter 1:4). You are a child God, held dear in the embrace of the Father, and the heir of great and precious promises. Allow the Holy Spirit to take over your thinking, and hear who you truly are in Christ.

Never place your identity in anything you can lose. One day, after getting ready for the day, I went downstairs, hugged Cheryl, and said, "Honey, I need to apologize to you." She pulled away, puzzled. "For what?" I chuckled, pointed to my wrinkled face and thinning gray hair, and said, "For all this. You didn't sign up to look at this every day, but here we are!" We both had a great laugh, and Cheryl said, "That's okay. I didn't marry you for your looks anyway. It was your money!" Humorous for sure, but there was a tinge of sincerity in my apology. After all, I had worked hard to win Cheryl, and back then, proving that I was a cool dude was part of the game.

It is so easy to connect our identity to things that will spoil and fade. We do it innocently, believing it will help us fill the deep longings of our lives. Combine naivete with need, and Satan has a heyday, convincing us that security comes through achievement.

I look back and see how deeply I invested in athletic abilities, relationships, possessions, degrees, title, and performance. I bought the lie hook, line, and sinker. Not one of those investments lasts forever. I can barely get off the floor when I kneel down, let alone score a goal or dunk a basketball. Any investment I made in my appearance is long overdrawn. Never place your identity in anything you can lose, because sooner or later, you *will* lose it.

Where have you attached your sense of security, significance, acceptance, purpose, and love? The Holy Spirit will help you detach from what spoils and fades and attach your longings to your identity as a child of God. God's provision for your life is eternal, rock solid, and life-giving. Achievement, on the other hand, will not only spoil, but its gifts are illusive. Even when you get what you so desperately seek, it soon becomes nothing more than dead weight.

Learn to practice the antirrhetic method, replacing the lies of the evil one with the Word of God. While the word *antirrhetic* is certainly uncommon, the meaning is relevant to the discussion of identity security as a child of God. It means, in its most elementary form, "to disagree, or to move in the opposite direction." As a method of dialogue, it involves refuting or countering a statement with an opposing viewpoint. So while you cannot stop intrusive and negative voices from entering your mind, you can resist those thoughts and not add your voice to their accusations. Learn to talk back to the voices that demean you by declaring what is true.

That is what it means to use the Sword of the Spirit against the evil one (Eph. 6:17). It is a great way to resist the voices of darkness and declare before heaven and earth what is true of you in Christ. When the voices in your mind intrude, make a counterargument! Speak the Word, out loud if necessary, repeating what God says about you in his Word. In the book of Ephesians alone are over fifty statements about who you are, true since the day you took your first step as a Christian.

Is there a specific demeaning statement that rolls in your mind? Dig into God's Word. Find the counterargument, and boldly declare what is true. Do you ever get beat up for things you have done in the past? Counter that with the promise that you are a new creation in Christ (2 Cor. 5:17). Have you ever been harassed with thoughts about being worthless? Declare that you are a masterpiece of God (Eph. 2:10).

Did someone once call you a "nobody" and that recording keeps playing in your mind? Shout back that you are seated with Christ in heaven and are the dwelling where God himself lives (Eph. 2:6, 22). People, the world, and the evil one can say what they may, but you are a child of the King. Learn to talk back and flow in the opposite direction.

Spend more time gazing at the One who is gazing back at you. One day when I was wrestling with my normal destructive thoughts, I received a small book from a friend. That very day I was stuck in the hog wallow of self-criticism, and the mailman delivered the gift *Union and Communion or Thoughts on the Song of Solomon*, by Hudson Taylor.

Most of what Hudson Taylor wrote passed through my mind like water through a sieve—except this line: "Well it is when our eyes are filled with his beauty, and our hearts are occupied with Him. In the measure in which this is true of us we recognize the correlative truth that His great heart is occupied with us."[4] Something happened as I read those words. God fills his eyes and heart with me? When I take time to gaze at him, can I discover that he is just as preoccupied gazing at me? Sounds too good to be true.

How we look at people, particularly children, impacts their self-worth and self-esteem. It is a fascinating thought and a great responsibility. Our facial expressions communicate so deeply that it registers in nanoseconds and goes straight to the emotions. To some degree, how you feel about me, expressed through facial expressions and tone of voice, can impact how I feel about myself. That's a whole lot of power to be wielding, often in a cavalier manner.

With that in mind, think about God gazing at you. There are plenty of scriptures that talk about God's face shining on his children. His gaze, at least in part, communicates that you are a beloved, chosen, and empowered child, secure under the watchful eye of the One who lavishly loves you.

There is an old adage that says, "Glance at your problems, but gaze at God!" What an amazing way to awaken your true identity as his child. Gaze at God gazing at you. How does that happen? Worship and praise more, allow the Holy Spirit to take over your imagination to help you experience the many truths of who you are in Christ, spend more time going to your safe place and resting with the Lord, and ask the Holy Spirit to help you experience the matchless presence of the Father, who has promised to love you, keep you, be gracious to you, and give you peace. Gaze at Jesus, and you may catch him looking back with longing love.

EXPERIENTIAL

The Holy Spirit delights in guiding you to your sacred space. Go there with him, quiet your heart, and get positioned for a present-moment encounter with the Lord. Ask the Holy Spirit to help you capture the gaze of God as he looks at you.

Remain in the Light

Read the following Scriptures as though written directly about you and to you. This is God's Word, holding promises and prayers that secure your identity as his child.

> But when the right time came, God sent his Son, born of a woman, subject to the law. God sent him to buy freedom for us who were slaves to the law, so that he could adopt us as his very own children. And because we are his children, God has sent the Spirit of his Son into our hearts, prompting us to call out, "Abba, Father." Now you are no longer a slave but God's own child. And since you are his child, God has made you his heir. (Gal. 4:4–7 NLT)

> My response is to get down on my knees before the Father, this magnificent Father who parcels out all heaven and earth. I ask him to strengthen you by his Spirit—not a brute strength but a glorious inner strength—that Christ will live in you as you open the door and invite him in. And I ask him that with both feet planted firmly on love, you'll be able to take in with all followers of Jesus the extravagant dimensions of Christ's love. Reach out and experience the breadth! Test its length! Plumb the depths! Rise to the heights!

Live full lives, full in the fullness of God. (Eph. 3:14–19 *The Message*)

Imagine Prophetically

Invite the Holy Spirit to take over your imagination. Ask him to use it to engage what Scripture says is true of you.

- Imagine yourself being set free from the burden of the law.
- Picture God sending the Holy Spirit into your heart.
- This translation says the Holy Spirit helps you cry "Abba, Father." Spend time crying out those words.
- What picture does the Holy Spirit want to give of you being a child?
- Allow the Spirit room to strengthen your inner being.
- What does having your feet firmly planted on love look like for you?

Notice

- Spend some time scanning your feelings. What emotions are arising as the Holy Spirit meets you in this exercise?
- Spend time with the verses from Galatians 4:4–7. What declarations can you make that will counter what the voices in your head are saying? Look for at least three.
- What did the Holy Spirit show you about being strengthened in your inner being?
- What feelings arise when you think of standing firmly on love?
- What can you declare about his extravagant love for you?
- What does a full life as a child of God look like for you?

Give Thanks

Use the scriptures above to shape a written prayer of thanks to your Lord Jesus. Once complete, share it with a friend you can trust.

NOTES

[1] Howard Thurman, *Jesus and the Disinherited* (Boston: Beacon Press, 1976), 50.

[2] Howard Thurman, *With Head and Heart: The Autobiography of Howard Thurman* (Orlando: Harcourt Brace and Co., 1979), 10.

[3] Thurman, *With Head and Heart*, 20–21.

[4] James Hudson Taylor, *Union and Communion with God or Thoughts on the Song of Solomon* (Lexington, KY: privately printed, 1894), 9.

16

AWAKENING TO GOD IN THE PRESENT MOMENT

In the movie *City Slickers,* a crusty old cowboy named Curly turns to a wisecracking urban executive and asks, "Do you know the key to life?" Curly holds up his gloved index finger and says, "One thing." The sarcastic Mitch asks, "So what's the one thing?" Curly replies, "That's what you've got to find out."

I remember when my dad's cousin took me on my first rabbit hunt and said something similar. He looked at me, a twelve-year-old kid, and said, "Do you know the key to being a good hunter?" Index finger extended into the air, he said, "One thing." After a long pause, he said, "Look for what shouldn't be there." I had no idea what he meant, but since he said it with gravitas, I nodded.

My coach in college got in on the act, asking before a game if we knew the key to victory. Arm held high, voice raised, face intense, and finger extended, he said, "One thing: leave it all on the field, play with determination, and be a team!" We glanced at each other and snickered. Even dumb jocks can count.

There is a story in the Bible about Jesus unexpectedly showing up at the home of Lazarus, which sent his sister Martha into a frenzy. She apparently scurried about, fixing beds and making sandwiches no one had ordered, while Mary, her sister, plopped onto the floor beside Jesus. Tension built until Martha turned on Jesus and said, "Lord, don't you care that my sister has left me to do the work by myself? Tell her to help me!" (Luke 10:40). Ouch!

Jesus gave Martha his own version of "one thing" philosophy. "Martha, Martha . . . you are worried and upset about many things, but few things are needed—or indeed only *one.* Mary has chosen what is better, and it will not be taken away from her" (Luke 10:41–42—emphasis mine). His one thing, which in fact may just be *the* one thing, boils down to this: be with God in the present moment.

Awakening to God in the present moment is the *unum necessarium* for a life well lived, the one thing necessary. God's kingdom is flowing all around you, his presence saturating the very air you breathe. Your problem is not the absence of God's presence, but the absence of *awareness* of his presence.[1] God is in this moment—and maybe you are not.

Distractibility and Other Bad Raps

Distraction is like a giant wall that blocks our experience of the Lord's presence. Our minds are often consumed by what has happened in the past and by what might happen in the future, seldom focused on what is happening moment by moment. I've come to call this "past/future focus," the description of a mind consumed by yesterday and tomorrow—and nowhere to be found in the present moment.

Do you play back yesterday over and over in your mind, chewing over past events like a dog worries over a dried-up bone? I do. Even if my thoughts leave yesterday for a few moments, they go straight to tomorrow, trying to anticipate how I will respond "if" or "when." I'm seldom fully present to what is going around me in the here and now. It's as if all my worries are knotted into a ball, moving back and forth in my mind between yesterday and tomorrow in a mental tennis match that has no end.

Jesus had me in mind when, in the Sermon on the Mount, he said, "Do not worry about your life. . . . But seek first his kingdom and his righteousness, and all these things will be given to you as well. Therefore do not worry about tomorrow, for tomorrow will worry about itself. Each day has enough trouble of its own" (Matt. 6:25, 33–34). This is sound spiritual and psychological advice, possibly more relevant today than when Jesus delivered this prescription two thousand years ago.

In his book *The Attentive Life: Discerning God's Presence in All Things*, Leighton Ford writes about a pilgrimage he took to Vancouver:

> It is a lazy midsummer afternoon, and I am alone on my spectator's perch except for a few ducks in the grass by the water's edge and some bicycle riders on the path behind me. Around the lagoon several couples are walking hand in hand.
>
> My eye is drawn to the fountain spouting up in the center of the lagoon; from there a flight of birds take off in perfect V-formation. They disappear, then in a few minutes come circling back, and still in formation splash down, their legs extended like the landing gears of seaplanes descending at nearby Cold Harbor. *Hmmm,* I think, *short flights and quick returns.*

As I watch their landing and muse on its symbolism, a seagull comes and sits just by my foot for a minute or two as if to say: "Pay attention now. This show is for you to notice."[2]

Have you ever missed the show? Was the present moment dealing up a full display of wonder, and you missed it? Have you ever complained that God never shows up for you, unaware that worry has placed blinders on your eyes?

Soon after reading Leighton Ford, I was sitting in a parking lot going over my notes for a new seminar. I was a bit nervous about how the material would go, especially since two hundred people had paid to attend. I was sitting in the driver's seat of my car reviewing my notes when I caught the movement of three Canadian geese walking single file in front of the car. I barely glanced. I'd seen geese before and needed to focus on what was coming up in less than an hour.

I went back to concentrate on my notes. Moments later, I noticed the three "visitors" had stopped directly in front of me, turned on cue, and looked at me as if I were a long-lost friend. I was about to blow the horn to send them scurrying along when the thought came: "Is this show for me?"

I decided to take a deep breath and enjoy the moment. A rather tender thought came to mind. "I wonder—is this God telling me the Trinity is with me and everything will be fine?" I smiled, and a feeling of contentment settled in upon me. As it did, the three visitors, again in single file, slowly walked out of sight. I closed my notes, rested in the present moment with the Lord, and moved on to a great time talking about Jesus with new friends.

Awakening to God in the Present Moment

Please let this thought go deep within your heart. God wants to fellowship with you. He is turned toward you, reaching for you, and longing to connect in intimate embrace. You are his cherished child. You matter to God.

God is not hiding from you, withholding his presence, or turned away because you did something wrong. He does not stand aloof waiting for you to prove yourself. He gazes at you in the present moment, wanting you to catch his glance and respond in love.

The movement of his kingdom does not reach back into yesterday, nor is God stepping into tomorrow to connect with you. *Now* is the moment to encounter him, when grace flows to your undistracted heart. Cry out to the Holy Spirit for awakening as you position yourself to meet the Lord. Remember the words of Jesus—seek first the kingdom, and when you do, everything else will fall into place. What follows are several practical steps that can position you for the gift of awareness.

Whenever you find yourself caught in past/future focus, ask the Holy Spirit to take over your thinking. Do you ever imagine the worst for tomorrow, allowing your thoughts to run wild with destructive speculation, then you become the victim of repeated worse-case scenarios that threaten to destroy your life? That is called *catastrophic thinking,* and there are times when I get trapped there. My mind obsesses with needless worry, and even worse, it seems impossible for me to step away from negative thoughts. They roll across my mind like a freight train carrying me to destruction.

God has no intention of meeting you in those thoughts. The enemy might, but not the Father. There is nothing "present moment" about sojourns into the land of needless anxiety and paralyzing fear, whether it consumes minutes or days of your life. Despite the fact that you may feel powerless to stop, God has made a way for you to come back to the present moment and be with him.

Cry out to the Holy Spirit, asking him to take over your thinking (Rom. 8:6). Whenever I start down that road, I try to take a few deep breaths, and then I repeat, "The mind controlled by the flesh is death. Holy Spirit, please take over my thinking." Even if you have to pray that repeatedly, stay in the rhythm of breathing and wait for the Spirit to bring you back to the present moment. When you surrender to his presence, the Holy Spirit will draw you back to what is true. You are his child, his love is lavish, he is watching over you with tender care, nothing takes him by surprise, and you are cherished. Allow these thoughts to center you.

Do things again for the very first time. When you do something for the very first time, you are aware of everything happening around you, almost hypervigilant, trying not to miss a thing. I'm teaching my sixteen-year-old granddaughter to drive. Yesterday, on one of the first lessons, she was "eyes wide open, white knuckle, slow the world down" attentive to everything going on around her. Every portal of information-gathering was active and on high alert. She was definitely in the present moment.

Sadly, that will not last. Once the driving neuropathways are set, she'll be going down the road eating pizza while talking to her friends with the radio full blast. It's the simple truth that once we experience things a few times, we become less attentive to everything happening. It moves us away from present-moment awareness, making a bit too much room for past/future focus.

Meeting the Lord in the present moment takes practice, and a great way to raise your attentiveness is by consciously slowing down to do common activities as if for the very first time. Sit outside facing the morning sun, close your eyes, and feel the warmth on your skin, listening attentively to the sounds around you as if you had never experienced the sun before. Eat an orange, peeling it back slowly, breathing in the fragrance as you open the skin. Taste a juicy wedge as if it were something you had never done before, and as you do, pay attention to what you are sensing, your feelings, and your body response in the moment.

There are a thousand small things you can do again for the very first time, and as you practice, you send a signal to your brain: "Pay attention—we don't want to miss the show." For the very first time, go on a walk, eat a salad, watch the sunset, kiss your spouse, smell flowers in the garden, hold a peach, listen to the stream, hear the rain as it falls on your roof. When you raise attentiveness in common moments, you position yourself to step into the present moment with God, and soon the present moment becomes filled with kingdom wonder.

Approach every present moment as a gift from God. While watching *Kung Fu Panda* with my grandchildren, I suddenly heard an amazing piece of wisdom from an animated turtle passing out sage advice to a bear overwrought by tomorrow's worries: "Yesterday is history; tomorrow is a mystery. Today is a gift, which is why we call it 'the present.'" I decided to try to run down the original quote, thinking it from some sage philosopher of years gone by. Not so. It showed up in the comic strip *Family Circus,* came from the mouth of Winnie the Pooh, and was even rephrased by a guy named Travis Dultz to read, "Yesterday is relative, tomorrow is speculative, but today is electric. That's why it is called 'current.'"

Regardless, whether it came from a cartoon character or blogger, the advice hits at the heart of mindfulness. God surrounds you with his presence every moment of every day (Acts 17:28). There is no mine so deep, no place so far out in space, no darkness so black, no storm so violent that he is not there.

Granted, the noise of the world and lies of the evil one will try to assault you like stormtroopers, but beneath it all is the quiet voice of God whispering, "Come to me, and I will give you rest." Every present moment is a gift from the Father. You need to enter that moment again for the very first time and find the gift waiting just for you.

Look for traces of God in everything he has made. God plays a cosmic version of *Where's Waldo?* daring you to find his presence in the world that surrounds you. The psalmist wrote that the world displays the majesty and craftmanship of God (Ps. 19:1–4). Present-moment awareness invites you to get out into creation, experience the majesty of God, and hear his voice. As Dallas Willard wrote, "Until our thoughts of God have found every visible thing and event glorious with his presence, the word of Jesus has not yet fully seized us."[3]

Each year, I required my doctoral students to bring a magnifying glass to class. After lectures on mindfulness and present-moment awareness, I sent them outside to "find God and hear what he has to say to you through creation." Initially, they rolled their eyes, convinced it was beneath such lofty scholars. Soon, they grew to love the experience and embraced it as a regular spiritual discipline. I would watch as they held a flower beneath the magnifying glass, examined a blade of grass, or looked deeply into the crevices of an open pinecone. Soon wonder emerged, and in the wonder was the voice of God. The heavens do indeed declare the glory of God.

A few years back, I hit a rough spot with my anxiety and set aside ten days to quiet myself before the Lord, asking for understanding and help. Soon I received God's prescription, which included more sunrises, more sunsets, quiet walks, naps in the sun, and an unleashed imagination that would draw me into the presence of God. Jesus saw the world as God-breathed and God-permeated, and he was inviting me to do the same.[4] Creation holds present-moment treasures. Go there often, alert to wonder, and when you do, you too may hear the voice of God.

Ask the Holy Spirit to give you an image that will help you trust God for tomorrow. There are times when picture language says it best, imbedding a truth into the soul through images rather than mere words. We learn through images as children. When a child associates the red plastic orb on the floor with the spoken word *ball,* the picture encodes in the brain. From then on, when "ball" is mentioned, the child does not see the letters b-a-l-l but the image that forever represents the reality itself.

An image has helped me return to the present moment when anxieties try to clog my throat. I attribute the experience to the Holy Spirit, who knows that mere words do not always go deeply with me but imaginative experiences of truth do. One day, as I was being assaulted by goose-stepping thoughts threatening to deliver the day's apportionment of doom, an image came to mind.

I was on a beach preparing to run into the ocean for a day of body surfing. Suddenly, I realized that my wallet was in my back pocket, holding my money, identification, credit cards, and family pictures. I dare not go into the water and damage those, and I saw no one around who I trusted enough to hold what was dear to me. So I merely waded along the edges of the water, barely getting my feet wet in the waves. Boring stuff.

The Holy Spirit began speaking to me through that image. He said that I often do not fully enter the moment with joy, because I am preoccupied with worry about so many things. I have, if you will, an imaginary wallet holding my health, my mental stability, and my reputation. Since I trust no one, I hold back in the present moment, afraid to be all in for fear of risking what is precious to me. The Holy Spirit showed me the Lord beside me on the beach, and he said, "Trust me with those. I'll take care of your health, your mind, your reputation. Go ahead—jump into today and have fun. I'll watch over what's important to you."

That image has served me well. Whenever anxiety rises, I return to the image and ask the Lord to hold my concerns while I jump in and play. Ask the Holy Spirit to open your prophetic imagination, so you too can enter the present moment with joy when worries try to threaten.

EXPERIENTIAL

The Lord waits to meet you in the present moment and longs to awaken you to his presence. I encourage you to simply say yes to his invitation. Prepare your heart and open your senses, taking in everything he longs to give you in the gift of this moment.

Remain in the Light

Invite the Holy Spirit to speak through God's Word today. It is the teaching of Jesus on worry from the Sermon on the Mount.

> If you decide for God, living a life of God-worship, it follows that you don't fuss about what's on the table at mealtimes or whether the clothes in your closet are in fashion. There is far more to your life than the food you put in your stomach, more to your outer appearance than the clothes you hang on your body. Look at the birds, free and unfettered, not tied down to a job description, careless in the care of God. And you count far more to him than birds.
>
> Has anyone by fussing in front of the mirror ever gotten taller by so much as an inch? All this time and

money wasted on fashion—do you think it makes that much difference? Instead of looking at the fashions, walk out into the fields and look at the wildflowers. They never primp or shop, but have you ever seen color and design quite like it? The ten best-dressed men and women in the country look shabby alongside them. If God gives such attention to the appearance of wildflowers—most of which are never even seen—don't you think he'll attend to you, take pride in you, do his best for you? What I'm trying to do here is to get you to relax, to not be so preoccupied with *getting,* so you can respond to God's *giving.* People who don't know God and the way he works fuss over these things, but you know both God and how he works. Steep your life in God-reality, God-initiative, God-provisions. Don't worry about missing out. You'll find all your everyday human concerns will be met. Give your entire attention to what God is doing right now, and don't get worked up about what may or may not happen tomorrow. God will help you deal with whatever hard things come up when the time comes. (Matt. 6:25–34 *The Message*)

Imagine Prophetically

- Invite the Holy Spirit to take over your imagination.
- Ask him to help you picture the things that often weigh you down in worry. Imagine they are in your hand, and take time to name them one by one.
- How do those worries consume your thinking?
- What impact does worry have upon you and what you are so concerned about?

- Has worry held you back from fully entering the present moments of life? If so, how?
- What would you do if Jesus extended his hand and said, "Let me hold those for you"?
- What would be different about your attentiveness to the present moment if he did?

Notice

Take some time to practice being attentive and alert. Choose to do something again for the very first time.

- What did you choose?
- What did you notice?
- What feelings arose as you did?
- How will this help you enter the present moment with the Lord?
- Go into creation today. God has hidden a treasure there. When you discover it, you will hear his voice.

Give Thanks

Please do not try to edit or censor your thoughts. Simply write a stream-of-consciousness psalm of thanksgiving about what you experienced in the present moment today.

NOTES

[1] Ronald Rolheiser, *The Shattered Lantern: Rediscovering a Felt Presence of God* (New York: Crossroad, 2004), 22.

[2] Leighton Ford, *The Attentive Life: Discerning God's Presence in All Things* (Downers Grove, IL: InterVarsity Press, 2008), 9.

[3] Dallas Willard, *Divine Conspiracy: Rediscovering Our Hidden Life in God* (San Francisco: HarperCollins, 1998), 62.

[4] Willard, *Divine Conspiracy*, 61.

17

AWAKENING TO YOUR SPIRITUAL GIFTS

G od has created a universe that is saturated with variety and diversity. "Everything from spiders to galaxies manifest the power of the Spirit" and display the wonder of God's creative genius.[1] Nowhere is this truer than with you.

You are not just another person occupying space on earth. You are a unique child of God, and as the adage goes, God threw away the mold after you were made. There is no one like you on the face of the earth, even if at this exact moment you are standing nose to nose with an identical twin. God invested a one-of-a-kind quality in you, ensuring that you are unlike any other human being who has ever lived.

Your DNA is 99 percent identical to that of every other person on earth. But that lone 1 percent makes all the difference in the world. One of my physician buddies told me that 1 percent represents millions of possible variations within the genome. Someone may look like you, dress like you, even use his or her fork the way you do, but there is only one you. Best of all, God is nuts about everything that makes you the person you are.

Diversity Matters

Ask most Christians what 1 Corinthians 12 is about and they will say spiritual gifts. That would be my answer as well. According to renown Pentecostal scholar Gordon Fee, that is only partially correct. According to Fee, the context of Paul's letter places the emphasis also on diversity.[2]

Paul in 1 Corinthians 12:4–6 describes an important creative tension. People have different gifts, and they are given by the same Spirit. There are different ways they can serve, but they all have the same Lord. There are different ways the Spirit works through people, but the same Spirit is doing it.

You have the same Lord, same Spirit, and same power flowing through you as every other child of God. At the same time, you are different from other believers. You have your own unique gifting, to be used in your own unique way, empowered by your own special anointing of the Holy Spirit.

I'm not sure why, but we can get tripped up believing that "real Christians" have an identical set of gifts, used in the same way, under a singular manifestation of the Holy Spirit, and anyone who falls short of those specs is delegated to the back row. Paul was upset with that kind of thinking, as revealed in his first letter to the Corinthian church. Folks were pushing tongues as the litmus test for spiritual moxie, and Paul wasn't having it. He started his discussion of spiritual gifts in 1 Corinthians by highlighting how much God loves *different* and how desperately the church needs *different* to be effective as the body of Christ in the world.

Gift projection is nasty, so it is important that you not allow anyone to force you into his or her mold. I have a colleague who was raised in Canadian Pentecostalism, and in his local church, tongues-speaking was evidence of God's stamp of approval. That didn't happen to be his gifting. The pressure was so intense when he was a teenager that he would mumble the names of the Iroquois tribes to satisfy people who were skeptical of his authenticity as a Christian.

I was my own victim of gift projection. I was blessed to be able to spend time learning from a man who had an amazing anointing from the Lord. It seemed as if heaven opened when he prayed and the Holy Spirit would move with great power. I wanted to minister like him, so I started asking God to give me that guy's anointing. One day, I sensed the Lord saying, "I did give you the same anointing. I gave you the anointing that matches my call on your life, the same way I gave him the anointing that best matched his calling." The anointing of God was the same, but the way it played out in my life was different.

That phrase, the same but different, may help you understand your place in the family of God. You are the same as every other Christian. You are a cherished child of God, and you have received all you need for life and godliness. Yet you are different. You have different gifts, to be used according to your own unique calling, with a specific anointing of power that matches your ministry of the kingdom.

The Holy Spirit Has Given You Spiritual Gifts

The day you came to Christ, you became part of an amazing movement that has been spanning the globe for centuries. God has placed you right at the heart of kingdom life, and I assure you that he didn't pass you by when the Holy Spirit was distributing spiritual gifts. You are a special person and able to do your part in a particular ministry to the world.

Clark Pinnock wrote,

> There had to be, after Jesus's departure, a colony of heaven, living the life and power and experiencing the freedom of the kingdom. Spirit indwells the church as a perpetual Pentecost and communicates gifts to its members. Spirit ecclesiology focuses not on the quality of its members but on the power of God at work in and through them.[3]

Stop selling yourself short. You are a key member of this colony of heaven. The power of God flows through you, as Pinnock said, in a perpetual Pentecost. You are a valued and needed member of the body of Christ, uniquely gifted to do your part in the ministry of Christ.

Are you able to see why the evil one is so determined to silence and sideline you? The dark harmony of voices has a clear agenda to diminish both who you are and what you are able to contribute to the ministry of the kingdom. The constant refrain demanding that you measure up is an all-out effort to keep you from discovering who you really are in Christ. But God is up to something special in you. You are equipped, through spiritual gifts, to play a critical role in his mission, and I'm sure you don't want to miss that grand adventure.

There is a word in Scripture that represents special endowments of grace placed in your life by the Holy Spirit for use within the body of Christ. That word in Greek is *charismata*, and "when specifically related to the activity of the Spirit, it seems to indicate some concerted ways in which the Spirit manifests himself in the believing community, granting them 'gracious bestowments' to meet the various needs and thus to build them up as the eschatological people of God."[4] I love Gordon Fee's phrase for spiritual gifts: "gracious bestowments."

The Holy Spirit has given you "gracious bestowments." Spiritual gifts are special channels of grace through which the power of God flows through you in order to build the church and minister to a broken world. It was not human competency that made the early church an effective force, but the power of God moving through ordinary people with extraordinary gifting from the Holy Spirit. Never hesitate to ask the Holy Spirit to do the same through you, awakening spiritual gifts and power in your life.

Discovering Your Spiritual Gifts

The Holy Spirit has not only gifted you, but he also wants to help you discover those gifts. If that interests you, then the best thing you can do is *read what the Bible has to say about spiritual gifts.* Did you know there are four chapters of Scripture that provide lists of spiritual gifts? They are Romans 12:3–8; 1 Corinthians 12:12–31; Ephesians 4:11–12; and 1 Peter 4:10–11. While these lists are not exclusive, they provide a great place for you to start your journey of discovery.

As you prayerfully read over the biblical list of spiritual gifts, *pay attention to your feelings.* There will be a natural interest, even affection for the "gracious bestowment" the Holy Spirit has placed in your life. I remember when Bob Miller, an elderly gentleman in our church, discovered that he did not have the gift of evangelism. For years he dutifully passed out gospel tracts, even went door to door sharing the gospel with folks. He was a faithful witness, but not particularly effective in evangelism.

As we began talking about being drawn to spiritual gifts, tears formed in his eyes. Bob said, "I've been trying to be an evangelist my entire life. The truth is, not only am I not very good at it—I don't like doing it." I asked, "What are you drawn to, Bob?" He replied, "I love to pray. I can pray all day and never get weary. Do you think intercession might be a gift?" The thought filled Bob Miller with joy, so we released him to do what he was made to do—and what he loved to do for Jesus.

Pay attention to your feelings. They may very well lead you right to the gifts the Holy Spirit wants to awaken in your life. Don't lean toward a particular set of gifts because someone told you they were the most important, or the ones given to spiritual superstars. That kind of pressure happens, but it never ends well for anyone.

Once you examine your feelings, *learn more about those spiritual gifts.* There are plenty of resources that can help, including books written specifically for that purpose. I know a number of people have been helped by Henry T. Blackaby's concise resource entitled *What's So Spiritual About Your Gifts?* And C. Peter Wagner's *Discover Your Spiritual Gifts.* There are also inventories and questionnaires available that may help you identify which gifts seem to fit your interests, personality, and natural talents. Try to find a Bible study on spiritual gifts, or a small group in your church where you can learn about spiritual gifts with other believers.

Sooner or later, you need to *step out in faith and give your gift a trial run.* In a safe, nonjudgmental context, experiment with the spiritual gifts that interest you. At first, you may experience that "Bambi on ice" sensation, but give it time. My first experience using my teaching gifts was a bumpy ride for me and for the folks listening. I had butterflies the size of flying dragons. I tried to jam way too much material down their throats right out of the gate, over-compensating for my feelings of insecurity.

Gratefully, my first foray into using my spiritual gift of teaching happened in a small group, among people who knew and loved me. Despite the rough start, something inside clicked, and I knew this was part of what I wanted to do the rest of my life. In time, with preparation and mentoring, and a whole lot of help from the

Holy Spirit, I sensed that I was made to teach, a "gracious bestowment" that has brought me joy for years.

Experimenting also showed me where I am *not* gifted. I am not so good at administration, do not shine at hospitality, and am pretty much a train wreck when it comes to saying just the right comforting words at the perfect time. While the Lord can use me in a pinch, I don't flow in prophetic gifting, have no known ability to interpret tongues, and seldom shine in gifts of service. That's okay with me. I love where the Lord has placed me in the body, because it fits who I am. Discovering spiritual gifting helped clarify God's will for my life, and I'm at my best right there.

Spiritual gifts are designed to advance the kingdom and build up the church. As you experiment with your possible spiritual gifts, *pay attention to the fruit.* Don't expect a hundredfold harvest the first week out, but sooner rather than later there should be evidence that the Holy Spirit has gifted you. For example, if you have the gift of evangelism, people should be coming to Christ through your ministry. If you believe you have the gift of healing, folks should improve as you minister to them.

Conversely, if you believe you have the gift of leadership but no one follows, or preaching and people go to sleep, or teaching and people get confused when you talk, maybe you need to look at other spiritual gifts. Knowing where I am *not* gifted is as valuable as discovering where I *am.*

On the journey of discovery, *allow the community of Christ to confirm your spiritual gifting.* If you hang out with God's people long enough, your spiritual gifting will leak out, sometimes even before you are aware you are gifted. People will be naturally drawn to your "gracious bestowments" and will begin leaning into your ministry. I have seen this happen many times. If people in my tribe need emotional support, they turn to Beth, if help problem-solving, they seek out Doug. When they need a solid dose of encouragement, folks end up on JoAnn's doorstep. Not one of them would put out a shingle advertising their gifting, yet the flow of the Holy Spirit attracts people to them as harbor lights do for the lost at sea.

Find some people who will pray over you regarding your journey of discovery. *Receiving prayer has a way of awakening your spiritual gifting.* When Paul sent his second letter to Timothy, he told him to keep alive his spiritual gifts that he received through prayer (2 Tim. 1:6). Find other members of the colony of heaven and have them pray over you.

Whenever I do a seminar on spiritual gifts, whether it's live or online, my team and I pray for people, asking the Holy Spirit to awaken their spiritual gifts. I ask them to stand for prayer as they sense the Spirit drawing them to a particular gift or gifts. At times we pray for them by the laying-on of hands.

Seeing the Holy Spirit awaken gifts in his people is one of the most exciting moments we have together at our seminars. The history of the church tells us that God has bound himself to his children through prayer. So find someone you know who takes prayer seriously, tell the person you want the Holy Spirit to awaken your spiritual gifts, and ask him or her to pray for you.

I was a caddy at Nottingham Country Club as a teenager. They were holding a club tournament over a weekend, and for whatever reason, I decided I was too tired to carry bags, so I stayed home. My plan was rest, lots of ice cream, and Western adventures with Roy Rogers and Trigger. Early Saturday morning, I was sound asleep in bed when my mother said I was wanted on the telephone.

It was the club pro at the country club, and he was upset. "Terry, where are you? This is the club championship. Get over here right now." There was no way I was moving. I was exhausted, and ten bucks for a double-bagger wasn't enough money to make me change my mind. The pro started laying on the pressure, when I heard, "Give me the telephone," in the background.

It was Mr. Vandenberg, a big deal in the community and one of the premier members at the country club. "Terry, this is Mr. V. I need your help. I have a chance this year, but frankly, I can't do it without you. What do you say? You in?" My heart about jumped through my chest, and in moments I was on my way. "I can't do it without you" was all it took, and for the next two days I did everything I could to see Mr. V win the trophy.

Which brings me to you. You are a member of "the colony of heaven" and you are here on earth for a purpose: advancing the kingdom of God. You are part of a vast community of believers who serve as the arms and legs of Jesus. You are called to take part in an amazing venture: turning what is ugly into something beautiful in Jesus's name. You offer unique gifts to this community, are endowed by the Holy Spirit with spiritual gifts, and anointed to bring light to a darkened world. "What do you say? We don't want to do this without you. Are you in?"

EXPERIENTIAL

The "beloved guest" is present in your life, always drawing you into deeper intimacy with Jesus. Stop for a while, allow quiet to settle around you, and listen to what the Holy Spirit wants to teach you about the "gracious bestowments" he has placed in your life.

Remain in the Light

Allow the Holy Spirit to be your teacher as you read the following scriptures.

There are different kinds of gifts, but the same Spirit distributes them. There are different kinds of service, but the same Lord. There are different kinds of working, but in all of them and in everyone it is the same God at work.

Now to each one the manifestation of the Spirit is given for the common good. (1 Cor. 12:4–7)

I want you to think about how all this makes you more significant, not less. A body isn't just a single part blown up into something huge. It's all the different-but-similar parts arranged and functioning together. If Foot said, "I'm not elegant like Hand, embellished with rings; I guess I don't belong to this body," would that make it so? If Ear said, "I'm not beautiful like Eye, transparent and expressive; I don't deserve a place on the head," would you want to remove it from the body? If the body was all eye, how could it hear? If all ear, how could it smell? As it is, we see that God has carefully placed each part of the body right where he wanted it.

But I also want you to think about how this keeps your significance from getting blown up into self-importance. For no matter how significant you are, it is only because of what you are a *part* of. An enormous eye or a gigantic hand wouldn't be a body, but a monster. What we have is one body with many parts, each its proper size and in its proper place. No part is important on its own. Can you imagine Eye telling Hand, "Get lost; I don't need you"? Or, Head telling Foot, "You're fired; your job has been phased out"? As a matter of fact, in practice it works the other way—the

"lower" the part, the more basic, and therefore necessary. You can live without an eye, for instance, but not
without a stomach. When it's a part of your own body
you are concerned with, it makes *no* difference whether
the part is visible or clothed, higher or lower. You give
it dignity and honor just as it is, without comparisons.
If anything, you have more concern for the lower parts
than the higher. If you had to choose, wouldn't you
prefer good digestion to full-bodied hair?

The way God designed our bodies is a model for
understanding our lives together as a church: every part
dependent on every other part, the parts we mention
and the parts we don't, the parts we see and the parts we
don't. If one part hurts, every other part is involved in
the hurt, and in the healing. If one part flourishes, every
other part enters into the exuberance. (1 Cor. 12:14–26
The Message)

Imagine Prophetically

Invite the Holy Spirit to be your teacher as you reflect on the
Scripture reading. Allow him to set apart your imagination as a
tool for communicating God's truth.

- Ask the Holy Spirit to help you see how you are different,
  yet the same.
- Allow him to reveal why *different* works best for advancing the kingdom.
- Invite the Spirit to help you visualize the "common good"
  he is working toward by distributing different gifts, service, and power.

- What has he shown you about the church being like a body?
- Ask him to reveal what part he wants you to play in the body of Christ.

Notice

- Where have you felt moved by the teaching on spiritual gifts?
- Notice your feelings as you consider your own spiritual gifting.
- Which gift or gifts are you drawn to?
- What is the Holy Spirit doing in and through you right now?
- Is there a desire growing for a new awakening to your spiritual gifting? If so, how do you intend to respond?

Give Thanks

Spend some time reflecting upon what the Lord has so deeply invested in your life through the Holy Spirit. Do you sense a new awakening happening? Gratitude would be an appropriate response to what God is doing in your cherished life.

NOTES

[1] Clark Pinnock, *The Flame of Love* (Downers Grove, IL: InterVarsity Press, 1996), 62.

[2] Gordon Fee, *God's Empowering Presence: The Holy Spirit in the Letters of Paul* (Peabody, MS: Hendrickson Publishers, 1994), 146–60.

[3] Pinnock, *Flame of Love*, 114.

[4] Fee, *God's Empowering Presence*, 35.

18

AWAKENING TO THE POWER OF COMMUNITY

We were working through one of my books in class when a student asked which section was my favorite. "That's easy," I said. "The dedication and the acknowledgments." Silence. Then a couple of snickers, a few grins, and from the rest, a human wall of blank stares.

"No, really. The dedication page is how I show gratitude to someone important to me. I like the acknowledgments at the end because I can say thanks to the people who made publication possible."

"Do you actually expect people to read that stuff?" another student asked.

"I assure you there will be no questions on the exam from the acknowledgments, if that's what you're asking." Smiles and exhales all around. Life again makes sense to everyone in the room.

I didn't get where I am today, whether for good or bad, without the influence of people who paid attention to me along the way. There is a legion of folks who prayed and stayed, extended a hand when I was too screwed up to reach out, and believed when only doubt swirled in my mind. There have been friends, family, colleagues, pastors, professors, coworkers, and unknown saints who patiently took me under their wing when life made little sense to me.

My name is boldly featured on the front of my books, as though I did it all by myself. That is not the case. It took dozens of people, including an agent, writing coach, several editors, marketing personnel, artists, communication coordinators, and a very kind and patient family who allowed the time to write.

My point? Acknowledgment is important. It's not just about honoring people. It's also a way to remember that I haven't made this journey alone. There is as much *we* to my story as there is *me,* true of anything I say, write, or do in my life. There is a name on the dedication page, Grandma Della Saunders. She stands as tall as a saint and gave me a place in her Jesus-loving heart. Recently, I had a chance to connect with her grandson, and we spoke about her undying impact on people's lives, not the least my own.

Whatever impact I may have had on others is in part linked to Grandma Saunders. Her name is not on the cover of a book, or the answer to a question on an exam, or known much beyond our little hometown of Finleyville, but that dear saint deserves an acknowledgment, and I am determined to give it. She is a reminder that it takes a community of love and care to change a life.

Psychiatrist and author Curt Thompson is on my life's acknowledgment page. He has taught me about friendship and the importance of community in a person's journey toward well-being and maturity. Curt, from the viewpoint of faith and science, knows that relationships make a difference in people's lives. Without healthy connection, the human mind is seldom at its best.

Curt writes,

> The mind is as relational as it is embodied. By this I
> mean that the very emergence of the mind's capacity to

do what it does is crucially dependent on the presence of relationships. From the day we enter the world, our neurons are firing not only out of the depths of genetically influenced patterns but also in response to the myriad of social interactions we sense and perceive when we encounter other people.[1]

We do not get through life successfully by ourselves. Relationships matter.

Acknowledgment needs to be added to the list of spiritual disciplines. Christian community is the context of our psycho–spiritual growth. We must recognize how much we need people, how much people need us, and why we are forever connected as the functioning body of Christ. We may be different and unique in gifting, service, and empowerment, but we are united as one by the love of Christ.

Paul urged us to maintain the unity of the Spirit through the bond of peace (Eph. 4:3). Given how horrendously divided people are across the globe, groups discriminating in ways that belie common sense and basic empathy, it is critical that the community of Christ awaken, revealing the love of God to the world and reconciling people to him.

The Trinity as the Foundation of Healthy Community

You are not the lone image-bearer. The gathered community of God's people is also a reflection of God. When we relate to one another with unselfish love, we reflect the relationship that exists eternally between Father, Son, and Holy Spirit. The world should be able to look at our corporate experience and remark, "Oh, how they love one another!" Mutual respect and affirmation not only reflect the best of Christian community, but they also model the harmony that exists within the Trinity.

Author Jean Vanier writes,

> More and more people are becoming conscious that
> our God is not just a powerful Lord telling us to obey
> or be punished but our God is family. Our God is three
> persons in love with each other; our God is commu-
> nion. And this beautiful and loving God is calling us
> humans into this life of love. We are not alone; we are
> called together to drop barriers, to become vulnerable,
> to become one.[2]

Reflecting God as family demands deep commitment and healthy vulnerability. We are human and as such we are broken. Since we are broken, we can easily become wounded wounders. Grace must be hardwired into the community, or people will go into hiding, or worse, strike out in their pain.

I was invited to speak on emotional healing, and the church suggested the title "Wounded in the Household of God." I asked what direction they intended me to take—wounded people who are now in the household of God, or those who have been wounded by the household of God?

I have over two decades of experience working with Christians who struggle with emotional wounds. How the wounded are treated determines whether people are vulnerable or whether they hide behind a mask of pretense. If the community of Christ is willing and open, treating one another with love and acceptance, we can awaken and experience the transforming power Jesus intends to flow through his people.

The Transforming Power of Community

If you're longing to be part of a community of believers who speak grace fluently and reflect the ecstatic dance of mutual love found in the Trinity, graciously evaluate that community's commitment to these three questions: Is the community Spirit-saturated, is the community a sanctuary, and is the community practicing scandalous acceptance?

We cannot function as a healthy community of Christ in our own strength. People must be open to the empowerment of the Holy Spirit from their first step on the way of Jesus to the last. The power of the Holy Spirit is the first evidence that the kingdom is at work in our midst and the guarantee of things yet to come. The only way to effectively follow Jesus is by the Holy Spirit. A healthy Christian community is then a Spirit-saturated community.

A healthy Christian community never relegates the Holy Spirit to a lesser member of the Trinity. The Holy Spirit is God with us, and dependence upon him is a mark of maturity, the key to being Christ's witness in the world (Acts 1:8). Christians often make plans, organize efforts, set strategies, and do the work of ministry with barely a nod to the leading or empowerment of the Holy Spirit.

I was praying before an event and said, "Lord, I promise to do my best." Immediately I sensed this: "Your best will not accomplish what I have in mind today." Effectiveness takes that perpetual Pentecost. The Holy Spirit must be active within the colony of heaven for the community of Christ to function as his body. While no community is perfect, the called-out and called-together must welcome the "beloved guest." A Spirit-saturated community is made up of broken people who stand shoulder to shoulder whispering, "Come, Holy Spirit."

Even as a young boy, I was captivated by the 1939 motion picture *The Hunchback of Notre Dame*, based on Victor Hugo's classic novel. The story takes place in France during the Middle Ages. Esmeralda is a beautiful young gypsy who captivates the hearts of the men in the community. When Quasimodo is flogged and turned on the pillory in the center of town, Esmeralda defies the authorities and brings him water, which saves his life.

Later, when Esmeralda is on the gallows, about to be hanged for a crime she did not commit, Quasimodo swings down on the bell tower rope and carries her off to the cathedral, shouting, "Sanctuary, sanctuary, sanctuary," sending the crowd into an uproarious celebration of joy. Watching that scene still gives me chills. How desperately the broken, bruised, and beat-up need the community of Christ to be a sanctuary to them!

Sanctuary is not simply a place of worship adorned with stained glass, candles, and a pipe organ. *Sanctuary* means a community where the wounded and accused can find refuge and protection from forces that want to do them harm. The community is a sanctuary when the people of Christ do not merely welcome the disenfranchised but go out, find them, stand up for them, and bring them into their embrace. Swinging down on the bell rope to rescue the accused is a symbol of the community of Christ at its best.

Moments before I was to preach at an inner-city church in Baltimore, three women performed an interpretive dance as part of the worship celebration. Dressed in flowing white dresses, they moved in harmony to the music of an African American gospel song about freedom and deliverance. It was stunning, almost angelic, as they used movement to proclaim the wonder of Christ. The pastor, sitting at my right, whispered, "They're heroin addicts. We rescued them from the streets, and now they belong to Jesus." Sanctuary, sanctuary, sanctuary!

Awakening to the power of community leads people away from condemnation and judgment and extends scandalous acceptance to the wounded of the world. Instead of public statements about who is unwelcome, *scandalous acceptance* means the church believes in human worth and dignity, treating people with respect regardless of how they live or the burdens they carry.

Gordon came to us dressed from head to toe as a woman. He was a wounded human being who told us about severe abuse as a child at the hands of an alcoholic father. Somehow he believed his clothing protected him. The community decided to let love win the day. Gordon was accepted into a small group, funded to get medical treatment, welcomed into full fellowship within the community of faith, and never pressured about changing his wardrobe.

Gordon began to heal and started a journey of self-discovery. Changes on the inside began to be reflected on the outside. Over time, Gordon didn't need to hide anymore from himself, from others, and from the past. Love surely does make a way. Scandalous acceptance, even when it looks as radical as eating with tax collectors and sinners, holds the power to transform us all.

Making Community Your Priority

You may have been wounded through relationships and wary of putting yourself out there again. Possibly you were hurt by the very people who were supposed to love you and keep you safe. I have regrettably been on the receiving and giving end of that kind of bad behavior.

Don't allow that to keep you from prayerfully and carefully awakening to the transforming power of community. Move forward with discernment. Accept the fact that we are going to bump into one another at times along the way. That's where mercy and forgiveness come to play.

If you do not have a local church, *look for a congregation fluent in grace*. Granted, no congregation will get this perfectly—just make sure they're on the journey. The congregation I pastored in California adopted an informal slogan: "It's okay not to be okay."

We tried to treat everyone with dignity and respect, regardless of how they came through the door. It got messy at times, but so does life. Years later when I had my own season in the ditch, I experienced just how transforming that stance can be.

Hopefully, the community you become a part of is filled with "journey" Christians, particularly among the leadership. If you spot a great deal of "box" church thinking, I would encourage caution. One thing is for sure: Jesus called you into community, and you need to be part of the called-out and called-together body of Christ (Heb. 10:24–25).

I especially encourage you to *find a small group of fellow travelers* who will gather around you in Christ's name. Jesus seems to have loved his small-group experience while on earth, so much so that he promised to show up when you hold your own gathering of two or three people (Matt. 18:20).

I have had experience with groups of every size, from congregations over a thousand, fellowship groups around a hundred people, and intimate gatherings of a handful. Unquestionably, the small group has been the most formative and supportive. When grace is in place, the small group becomes a place of acceptance, healing, learning, and transformation. To this day, every other week I meet with a small group of people who have no other reason to be together than for gathering around Jesus to experience adventures in the kingdom.

Having a good spiritual friend is also a great way to awaken to the power of community. Each of us needs someone who accepts us as we are but whose love never leaves us that way. That has been Evan. For several decades, whether we are together or oceans apart, I have felt safe with Evan, and valued. He became my friend before I stepped onto the path and has remained there through thick and thin. He has spent his life as a missionary to the world—and to me.

You need to find one or two relationships in which you are free to say what's on your mind, share your thoughts even when they are unruly, be rowdy when it overtakes you, and gut-level honest about your struggles and weaknesses—a couple of friends who are safe enough to bring along to your private Gethsemane and mature enough to hear you pray, "God, is there any other way?" You need someone who values failure and prioritizes grace.

One other investment can awaken you in wonderful ways: *Find a gifted spiritual director* and spend time meeting Jesus in the story of your life. Spiritual direction is an age-old practice that is gaining traction today. It is the process of helping you discover God in the sacrament of the present moment. A spiritual director is not there to solve your problems, like a counselor, or to advise you on how to handle a challenge, like a coach. He or she helps you discover what God is doing in your life so you can respond appropriately.

Most spiritual directors will spend time focusing on two things. First, they will introduce you to spiritual disciplines that help raise your awareness to the presence of God. My spiritual director has shared several prayer exercises that increase my ability to be present in the moment. A good spiritual director chooses what best fits your journey, helping you respond to the whispers of God as he engages your daily life.

Second, spiritual directors will help you look at a current struggle or challenge, never asking how it happened or what you intend to do, but propose questions that help you discover what God is up to and how that challenge can be used to change your life. Recently, I experienced some opposition that began to stir up anger in me. After all my moaning and complaining, my spiritual director asked two simple questions: "Where is God in this?" and "What is God wanting to shape in your life?"

Choosing a spiritual director is a matter of prayer and discernment. You would also do well to do some research discovering who is available, what their qualifications are, and who recommends them. I assure you: if the Lord leads you to invest in this type of relationship, it is usually, over time, a great way to awaken your spiritual life.

I'm sure you can list many reasons, both practical and personal, that connecting deeply with people can be a challenge you'd rather not face. I understand. Allow me to suggest one reason that makes all those arguments moot. The community of Christ is the face of God in the world today, each member adding power to its witness. Awakening to the power of community is in part awakening to the power you bring to community. We are better with you than we are without you. The community of Christ needs you.

EXPERIENTIAL

Jesus once said to his disciples, "Come with me by yourselves to a quiet place and get some rest" (Mark 6:31). *Rest* did not mean a nap but rather a season of renewal and refreshment with Jesus at the center. Approach this experiential as that invitation, a time to step away from the noise of your life and into the presence of the Lord. Position yourself to best experience him in the present moment.

Remain in the Light

The following scriptures hold promises and instructions related to awakening to the power of community. Ask the Holy Spirit to reveal the word he wants to bring to you from his inspired Word.

Two are better than one,
    because they have a good return for their labor:

If either of them falls down,
>   one can help the other up.
But pity anyone who falls
>   and has no one to help them up.
Also, if two lie down together, they will keep warm.
>   But how can one keep warm alone?
Though one may be overpowered,
>   two can defend themselves.
A cord of three strands is not quickly broken.
>   (Eccles. 4:9–12 NLT)

I beg you—I, a prisoner here in jail for serving the Lord—
to live and act in a way worthy of those who have been
chosen for such wonderful blessings as these. Be humble
and gentle. Be patient with each other, making allowance
for each other's faults because of your love. Try always
to be led along together by the Holy Spirit and so be at
peace with one another.

We are all parts of one body, we have the same Spirit,
and we have all been called to the same glorious future. For
us there is only one Lord, one faith, one baptism, and we
all have the same God and Father who is over us all and in
us all, and living through every part of us. (Eph. 4:1–6 TLB)

Imagine Prophetically

The passage from Ecclesiastes is filled with prophetic image. Quiet
yourself and invite the Holy Spirit to help you engage the text with
your imagination and your senses, taking the truth beyond understanding to *knowing*.

- What image does the Holy Spirit bring to your mind
  when showing you that two are better than one?

- Ask him to provide a picture of you falling alone, then a picture of you falling and someone helping you up.
- Picture being back to back in battle with someone.
- Imagine the cord of three strands.

Notice

- Always begin noticing by paying attention to your feelings. What did you notice as you read and imagined these scriptures?
- Have you ever fallen alone? What was that like?
- Has anyone picked you up along the way? Who, when, why—and what did that teach you?
- Who makes up your cord of three strands?
- Notice these terms from Ephesians 4:1–6: *Humility, gentleness, patience, bearing in love,* and *the bond of peace* (ESV). What impact do they have on community?
- What do the following terms tell you about community? *One body, one Spirit, one hope, one Lord, one faith, one baptism, one God and Father.*
- What commitments are you ready to make concerning your movement toward community?

Give Thanks

Make your own list of acknowledgments. Who has helped shape your walk with Jesus? Have you told him or her lately? Have you thanked the Lord for placing this person in your life?

NOTES

[1] Curt Thompson, *The Soul of Shame: Retelling the Stories We Believe about Ourselves* (Downers Grove, IL: InterVarsity Press, 2015), 40.

[2] Jean Vanier, *From Brokenness to Community* (Mahway, NJ: Paulist Press, 1992), 35.

19

AWAKENING TO YOUR TRUE SELF

All creation waits. What a stunning image! It brings to mind the moment when, at a grand wedding, the entire gathering awaits the entrance of the bride. The groomsmen face the back watching for her arrival. The groom focuses his gaze to the rear of the church, anticipating the moment when his beloved will step into view in all her splendor. He has never seen her as she will now appear, this first glimpse forever framed in his mind.

The music builds, the bridesmaids stand to the side as a backdrop, and the bride comes into view. People rise to their feet as one, eyes only upon the bride. The ceremony that follows is important, but this is the moment that captivates their imagination. The bride steps into full view, more beautiful than imagined. The room comes alive with smiles and tears and whispers about her beauty. Everything has been leading up to this great unveiling, her first steps into the life she now gets to live.

All creation waits. Those words birth a thousand thoughts, each bursting forth with images of celebration and breathtaking movement, captivating anyone and everyone who even catches a glimpse. It's parents seeing their newborn for the first time, a wife watching her husband step off an airplane after years of separation caused by war, the wonder that fills a parent watching a child's first steps, hearing a doctor say, "She's going to be fine," a treasure uncovered as the last leaf is turned, and the scene of a miner trapped beneath the earth, long thought dead, emerging from the ground like Lazarus from the tomb. *All creation waits.*

This phrase, as stunning as it is, was written in part about you. It reads, "For all creation is waiting eagerly for that future day when God will reveal who his children really are" (Rom. 8:19 NLT).

What you have read in this book, every experiential that you have completed, each scripture that you have pondered, were all moving toward this moment of awakening. You are a wonder, filled with unique gifting and brilliance, and all creation waits for the real you to step forward. All creation watches with anticipation for your true self to awaken, so that you might shine like stars before the world, a testimony to the glory of God and the transforming power of Christ (Phil. 2:15).

The Projected Self

There are many reasons you have suppressed your true self. In part it's the pressure the world applies trying to force you into its mold rather that helping you release God's image to the world. The attack from the evil one, aimed at your true identity, may have been subtle, but it is always relentless, seeking to steal, kill, and destroy. Christians who have suggested that discipleship begins with who you need to become, rather than who you are in Christ, have not helped. Then, of course, there are your own choices, motivated by the angst of unmet longings, twisting desire away from God, inviting idols of the heart to occupy a space only God can fill.

If your true self was suppressed, how then did you relate to the world? While many people refer to a dichotomy between the true self and false self, I find it unhelpful. Wanting to get what we need for life, we develop what I would call a "projected self"—the self we believe acceptable to the world in which we live, and necessary to advance and survive in a performance-based culture; the self we want people to think we are, projected in order to get and gain control. This projected self is an accommodation to the dark voices that say you are not enough, the result of pressure to perform in order to have your core longings met.

The projected self, the way you present yourself to the world, is not something false about you, but rather a misuse of what is true, manipulated for selfish purposes. You take something true and use it dysfunctionally as part of the maladaptive projected self, all to get what you want. The projected self is driven by genuine desire but flows in pretense and self-protection, all designed to provide for yourself. The projected self is a limited, selfish, and unhealthy misuse of who you really are.

My own wounds and insignificance drove me to develop a projected self, though I had no idea that was what I was doing. I wanted to survive in the world, find a place for myself where I mattered, where I belonged, and where I was safe. I took aspects of my abilities, passions, talents, and gifts and manipulated them to serve my purposes. I brought part of myself to the surface and hid other parts, based on whatever got me accepted or met my needs. God gave me gifts because I was his child, but disconnected from him, I took pieces of what he gave in order to selfishly promote myself. I projected the self I wanted the world to see, all the while diminishing myself in the process.

Parker Palmer writes, "We arrive in this world with birthright gifts—then spend the first half of our lives abandoning them, or letting others disabuse us of them."[1] I have experienced this, and I am sure you have as well. We may have done it subconsciously, but the effect has been the same. We stepped away from the true self, focusing on the values of the world and whoever it expected us to be. For a while it worked, as with any other addictive behavior. But the day comes, not necessarily at the halfway point of life, when the projected self begins to crumble, and we are faced with a choice. Will we awaken to the wonder of our true self, or will we spend the rest of our life killing the pain that remains because desire was never fulfilled?

There are moments in time, seasons on the journey of Christ, when God beckons us to awaken. He tenderly summons us from our sleep with gentle wooing, the sweet invitation to step more fully into life. If we fail to stir, he will wrestle us awake. When necessary, a severe mercy is extended from the Father's heart. He is determined to set us free so that we might thrive in the gifts of grace. Even a trip to a psychiatric hospital can be the hand of God reaching out to my true self and inviting me to dance.

When Good Gifts Are Misused

I was always fascinated watching my father's hands when he was working with a tool. After his spending forty years as a mechanic in the coal mine, a tool became an extension of his body. He would choose the exact tool, hold it at perfect angles, apply pressure precisely where and how it was needed. He never fumbled with it or allowed it to twist in his calloused hands. The tool seemed at home there, submitting to Dad's will, not because of brute force but rather an almost mystical connection between them. I tried to mimic Dad after watching him use a channel lock wrench. The tool and I never became one.

One day, long after I was married and had kids, I went into my workshop to get something to pound a nail into the deck behind the house. Dad was there and watched me begin to hammer a six-penny nail into a plank with a crescent wrench turned sideways. Two whacks and a bent nail later, Dad became animated. "What are you doing? You're going to ruin it!"

"Ruin what? It's one nail. This thing is made of steel—it can take it."

"Give me that. You keep that up and you'll ruin a perfectly good tool. You've already bent the nail and you're probably going to bust the board. That's not how you treat a tool like this. Get a hammer. It's made for the kind of pounding you're doing—this is not. These things cost money!" I never liked Dad's lectures, but he was right. Good things used improperly can create a lot of damage and never get the job done correctly.

God filled you with good gifts, and they are for specific purposes, every one meant to benefit your life and serve the advancement of his kingdom. He does not want those gifts to remain hidden or manipulated for self-centered purposes. I've done that, and it has never ended well. The Lord instilled strength in me, which, when operating from my true self, can serve people in Christ's name. However, insecurity led me to take that strength and use it to intimidate, to get my will, to meet my own selfish needs.

The Lord also gave me the ability to figure things out, to see chaos and find the order inherent within it. Instead of using that gift to help other people journey though the storm, I used it to get a place at the table, to secure my own position of importance and power. Am I pleased that I used myself in such a selfish way?

Absolutely not. Good gifts, used in bad ways, even when motivated by legitimate desire, stifle the true self. It results in a self-centered existence as opposed to releasing the wonder of the centered self.

Awakening the True Self

You have come a long way on your journey of awakening. You have positioned yourself before the Lord and experienced the truth of who you are in Christ. Your identity is not focused upon what is broken but upon being the beloved. You have learned about being a wonder, an image-bearer, and a new creation in Christ Jesus. You are far more equipped to resist the evil one and push back against the world's claim that you are not enough. Instead of being beat down with a harsh gospel, you have said yes to the good news of the kingdom that flows into your heart with lavish love and extravagant grace.

How wonderful it must be for you, as it is for me, knowing that the "beloved guest" abides within you, calling you the loved, chosen, and empowered child of God! The present moment has become sacred space as the presence of the Father surrounds your life in the here and now. Secure in your identity, you are now free to unleash spiritual gifts into the community of Christ, not out of selfish gain but because you are wanted and needed on this grand adventure with Jesus.

All this growth, every experience you have had, and all you have learned converges, challenging you to say yes to the awakening of your true self. Your Father invites you to step forward into who he intended you to be since the foundation of the world. The awakening of your true self is a journey over time, in which moments in time become the place of self-discovery. As the hidden you emerges and the projected you surrenders, the wonder of the real you unfolds as a gift to the world.

Thomas à Kempis, a fifteenth-century Christian theologian, once wrote that there is no knowledge more profitable to a person than self-knowledge.[2] Only by knowing yourself can you yield yourself more fully to God as a cherished child, secure enough to serve rather than be served, to give instead of receive, to lay down to benefit others rather than gather to secure yourself. Is it any wonder that all creation waits for the children of God to be revealed? Your uniqueness and gifting, emerging from the awakening of your true self, bring the light of God into a darkened world.

Never underestimate the role love plays in the awakening of the true self. I look back upon my life and see that love was working even when I didn't know love was at work. Expressions of love great and small across the years have called out for me to awaken. Invariably even the smallest of gifts from people who cared found their rooting in the love of God, lavishly given because I was his child (1 John 3:1). I may not have noticed this love as love, but it noticed me, and it notices you. Love is the oxygen that nurtures your true self. Breathe it in deeply. Thomas à Kempis wrote:

> Nothing is sweeter than love, nothing stronger, nothing higher, nothing wider, nothing more pleasant, nothing fuller or better in heaven or earth "because love is from God" (1 John 4:7). Love flies, runs, and leaps for joy. It is free and unrestrained. Love knows no limits; it transcends all boundaries. . . . Increase this love in me, that in my innermost being I may taste the sweetness of your love. . . . Let me love you more than myself, and love myself only in you.[3]

Secure in God's love, ultimately expressed at the cross of Christ, you can say yes to the awakening of your true self. *With the Holy Spirit's help, begin with self-acceptance.* Make peace with your past and with any weakness with which you struggle. It is easy to look back at the mistakes of yesterday with unhealthy regret. Self-condemnation and self-judgement rise within, especially when the evil one joins his voice to ours.

This is a ditch into which I too often fall. There are a whole lot of "I sure wish I hadn't" moments in my past. The problem is not that I shouldn't take past sin seriously, but rather that I haven't taken the Lord's forgiveness more seriously. You must remember that Jesus has forgiven and cleansed the past, and the Father has promised that such sins no longer come to his mind, for he remembers them no more (Heb. 8:12). Instead of getting weighed down with what happened yesterday, rejoice that you are free to step into your true self today.

There may be more than a few places where transformation is still needed, where weakness from time to time tosses you to the ground. Look to Jesus, not only for strength but as a model of how to treat yourself. How did Jesus treat Zacchaeus, the woman at the well, the Gadarene, or the woman caught in adultery? He extended mercy, not condemnation. Mercy cuts a better path toward change than judgment (Rom. 2:3–4). If you begin with acceptance, your true self will be safe to emerge from hiding.

Acceptance does not mean there isn't work to be done in your life. It simply lays a better foundation for change than judgment. *Allow the Holy Spirit to raise your awareness of places in your life where investments in change will pay high dividends.* Give the Spirit room to show you where you are still responding to the world out of your projected self instead of the awakening true self.

It is easy to be blinded by our maladaptive systems of control. Neuropathways formed over the years make functioning out of the projected self as automatic as closing your eyes when you sneeze. It takes the Holy Spirit to help you step back and take notice of the self-centered ways you respond in life. It is possible to operate with a log in your eye and not even know you have a problem (Luke 6:39–42).

Awareness is about knowing yourself better, discovering how you relate to the world when unmet desire grips you. It is about inviting the Holy Spirit to show you where systems of control, manipulation, dysfunction, and dependencies are robbing you of freedom. They are weights keeping your true self from soaring. Ask the Holy Spirit to set you free so that you can live out of who you truly are in Christ. You are awakening, and self-awareness is a great ally on your journey of discovery.

Self-awareness serves the awakening of the true self, but you must be willing to go more deeply. *You need to discover the unmet longings that drive your projected self to act out in the first place.* Contrary to what people may think, there are motivations, conscious or subconscious, driving everything we do, every decision we make, and every gift or talent we choose to twist to our purposes. Becoming aware of what you do to control and manipulate your world is important, but discovering why you make such choices is far more important.

It was one thing for me to finally admit that I can get intense when confronted by someone, but another to find out why. The easy answer is that I do it to exercise control, but the question remains as to why that matters. The Holy Spirit gently revealed that my reactivity was rooted in a deeply held belief that I am fundamentally unsafe. Such insecurity births hypervigilance, so at the first sign of threat, perceived or otherwise, I swell up ready for a fight. The only way to be safe, I have falsely believed, is to dominate. I misuse God-given strength to my purposes.

Such behaviors can be rooted in old wounds. Freedom begins with awareness of what you do, followed by the Spirit-driven examination of why you do those things, and then the healing of unprocessed emotional wounds that may keep the true self in bondage to the past. Each step in that process is part of the journey to freedom, a journey that has already begun for you.

In all of this, there is a stance that does not come easily but is essential to the process of awakening. *Surrender, not achievement, opens the door for the Holy Spirit to awaken your true self.* When I was a boy, my mother occasionally took my sister and me to church, where the pastor, Sunday after Sunday, preached, "You must be born again." As his sermon drew to a close, the choir began to sing the Judson Van DeVenter song "I Surrender All."

Men and women would step from their pews, move to the front of the church, and kneel at the rail to meet Jesus. It was a turning point for them, pivoting away from the world and into the arms of Christ. Even as a boy I found it moving. The words *I surrender all* never felt like defeatism, but victory, as though the weight of sin fell away, and they could start living.

Surrender does not mean giving up as much as it does giving in to the work of the Holy Spirit. It is not an angry "Do what you want" but a prayerful "I want what only you can do." Surrender is a willingness to kneel before the Lordship of Christ and be set free to live fully out of who you are in him.

There is wonder in surrender, like the beauty that surrounds a person when he or she falls back into the waters of baptism, and is then brought up dripping wet with the cleansing power of Jesus. Surrender is that deep "Go ahead, Jesus—awaken me." It is the grand paradox, becoming Christ's captive in order to be free, surrendering up your sword, to stand as a conqueror with Jesus.[4]

You have been on a journey for some time now. You have learned, you have experienced, and now you have the opportunity to say yes to a lifetime of awakening. As this book comes to a close, it is only the end of a great beginning. You are a cherished child of God, filled with wonder. Say yes to the journey of self-discovery, and allow the Holy Spirit room to awaken every bit of your uniqueness and your gifting, all to the glory of the kingdom. There is a brilliance in you, a light reflected from the heart of God upon an image-bearer who is known before the throne as *beloved.* The Lord extends his hand to you. Take it, and step more fully into the light of who you are in Christ.

All creation waits!

NOTES

[1] Parker Palmer, *Let Your Life Speak: Listening for the Voice of Vocation* (San Francisco: Josey-Bass, 2000), 12.

[2] Thomas à Kempis, *The Imitation of Christ*, annotation by Paul Wesley Chilcote (Woodstock, VT: Skylight Paths, 2012), 5.

[3] Kempis, *The Imitation of Christ*, 83, 85.

[4] A paraphrase from George Matheson's nineteenth-century hymn "Make Me a Captive, Lord."

ACKNOWLEDGMENTS

As I finished speaking at a gathering called the "Warrior Connection Experience," the host presented me with a stunning piece of broken pottery repaired through the Japanese art form called Kintsugi. The broken pieces of the bowl had been bonded together with gold, and instead of hiding the imperfections, the process highlighted the fractures and made the bowl even more beautiful. It was the first time I had seen Kintsugi art and I was moved by how it illustrated my journey with the Lord. I held in my hands a symbol of the movement from broken to beloved.

Kintsugi means "golden repair" and has been practiced by artisans in Japan for over four hundred years. For centuries it has served as an artistic reminder that even through difficulty people can heal and grow and in the end more perfectly reflect the dignity God has placed in every human being. Kintsugi represents the biblical promise that "all things work together for good" when placed in the hands of God (Romans 8:28), even our brokenness.

I want to thank Greg Jackson with ThinkPen Design for creating a cover that reflects the art form of Kintsugi, providing a stunning visual of the journey from broken to beloved. Greg's artwork represents what I hope this book will say to its readers, and for that I am deeply grateful.

I love working with the people from Leafwood Publishers. Our relationship reaches back twenty years and has included several of my books. They have become cherished friends. I especially want to acknowledge the hard work and support of Jason Fikes, Duane Anderson, and Mary Hardegree. It has been fun to once again work together. May our dear Lord bless you and the Leafwood family richly.

This book would not have happened had it not been for my agent, Ann Spangler. In a vulnerable moment, I spoke to Ann about the tragic loss of a cherished life, wishing that dear and precious person could have seen the wonder we all knew was present within her. From that, Ann drew from me the narrative arc that has become this book, believing there may be others who need to discover that God has shaped them as image-bearers, matchless creations of his eternal art. Only our Lord could have linked me with such a gifted, sought-after, and insightful person as Ann. I am forever grateful.

I have been on the journey long enough to know that the terrain cannot be successfully navigated alone. There are too many people who have walked with me to name here. I do want to thank the Healing Care Ministry Family. They are a tribe of seekers, moving forward shoulder to shoulder on the journey from broken to beloved. As I have said many times, I can't believe I get to walk the way of Jesus with each of them.

I want to thank the Saunders and Spearman families for honoring me with permission to dedicate this book to Grandma Saunders, as well as allowing me to mention her several times throughout the book. Brian Spearman, the grandson she raised, has been a cherished friend since childhood. It is through Brian that Grandma ended up impacting my own journey with Jesus. My affection for this family runs deeply, and I am humbled to honor so fine a saint as Della Saunders.

Mom and Dad are with Jesus now, and it brings me great delight imagining them alive in the kingdom that has no end. I am grateful that our journeys ultimately merged at the cross of Christ. Thanks go to my sister, Bonny, who has forever supported me with unconditional love, and who, in the early stages, read the manuscript, making encouraging comments while cheering me on.

To my son, Aaron, and daughters, Cara and Emily, I owe more that I can express in these few words. You bring light to my life in ways incomprehensible and indescribable. The fact that I get to walk this journey with each of you is grace beyond words. You are stunning image-bearers, filled with wonder still being unleashed. I see the face of God shining through your lives and I am continually undone. Destry, my daughter-in-law, is one of the most gifted counselors, caregivers, and teachers I know. Even more impressive is her presence, which I delight in as a proud father-in-law. Thanks also to my two sons-in-law, Brad and Micah. I love the way you love my girls and grandchildren. You bring strength to our family, and I am proud that I get to call each of you "Son."

I am sure all grandparents feel this, but Cheryl and I are convinced that we have the best grandchildren in the world. They are bright, beautiful, creative, and loving. Each of them brings unspeakable wonder to our lives. It is my prayer that Grace, Addison, Kayla, Caleb, Isabella, and Charlotte live knowing that Grandma and Papa are nuts about them. May they see in our smiles the reality that they are God's masterpieces, beloved eternally as his cherished children.

Finally, and with deepest gratitude, I want to thank Cheryl, my wife, my first and forever love. What a journey we share, far more exciting than we could have imagined when, over fifty years ago, I sat beside her on the school bus and asked her on a date. That moment began the great adventure, filled with the ups and downs of life that have mended our lives with the gold of God's healing grace. I not only thank you for reading the many drafts of this book, but also for being at my side as we seek to walk the way of Jesus. I adore you. How is it that, as the years go by, you look more stunning than that day, so long ago, when I first saw the light of your beautiful face? It is clear: I am a man most blessed.

If you, or someone you know, wants to begin a journey of healing, please consider Healing Care Ministries, where gifted and qualified caregivers offer Christ-centered counseling and care through a variety of personalized opportunities, as well as special seminars and programs that can lead you deeper as a follower of Christ. Contact information is available at https://healingcare.org.

I do a weekly podcast intended to provide helpful insights on the Christian journey. It is called *Slingstones*, available through a variety of podcast services, and is accessible through

https:terrywardle.com or
https://www.facebook.com/terry.wardle.3/